GOD'S WOODSHED

GOD'S WOODSHED

by
Stanley Tam
with
Ken Anderson

Horizon Books
3825 Hartzdale Drive
Camp Hill, PA 17011

Horizon Books
3825 Hartzdale Drive, Camp Hill, PA 17011

ISBN: 0-88965-095-0

97   98   99   00   01   7   6   5   4   3

Cover painting by Brenda Wintermyer

Contents

FOREWORD

Stanley Tam, of Lima, Ohio, has been my appreciated friend for thirty years. During that time we produced two motion pictures and released two books. These three decades have offered ample opportunity for me to evaluate the measure of Stanley Tam.

He is, to be sure, as human as every other mortal. What makes him exceptional and significant is a certain process he has discovered: how to become a functioning and productive child of God.

He would be the first to ask for no applause, no citations and no commendation.

However, he has indeed learned how to obey God, and he deeply desires to share these insights with others.

Thus this book.

God's Woodshed documents Stanley Tam's experiences in his quest for valid discipleship. It details the important role Divine discipline plays in the development of a follower of Christ. It is also a book designed to help others gear their lives to the biblical caliber of genuine holy living.

As you read, as you share this man's spiritual adventures, be on the watch for like drama to occur in your own life.

For surely it can!

Ken Anderson
Warsaw, Indiana

PREFACE

Psalm 51, with its account of David confessing his sins to God, provides the scriptural basis for *God's Woodshed*. Before reading the book, be sure to read this Psalm. It offers great insight into the power of a cleansed life!

PSALM 51

Have mercy on me, O God, according to your unfailing love; according to your great compassion blot out my transgressions. Wash away all my iniquity and cleanse me from my sin.

For I know my transgressions, and my sin is always before me. Against you, you only, have I sinned and done what is evil in your sight, so that you are proved right when you speak and justified when you judge. Surely I was sinful at my birth, sinful from the time my mother conceived me. Surely you desire truth in the inner parts; you teach me wisdom in the inmost place.

Cleanse me with hyssop, and I will be clean; wash me, and I will be whiter than snow. Let me hear joy and gladness; let the bones you have crushed rejoice. Hide your face from my sins and blot out all my iniquity.

Create in me a pure heart, O God, and renew a steadfast spirit within me. Do not cast me from your presence or take your Holy Spirit from me. Restore to me the joy of your salvation and grant me a willing spirit, to sustain me.

Then I will teach transgressors your ways, and sinners will

turn back to you. Save me from bloodguilt, O God, the God who saves me, and my tongue will sing of your righteousness. O Lord, open my lips, and my mouth will declare your praise. You do not not delight in sacrifice, or I would bring it; you do not take pleasure in burnt offerings. The sacrifices of God are a broken spirit; a broken and contrite heart, O God, you will not despise.

In your good pleasure make Zion prosper; build up the walls of Jerusalem. Then there will be righteous sacrifices, whole burnt offerings to delight you; then bulls will be offered on your altar.

1

God's Woodshed

God disciplines us for our good, that we may share in his holiness.

Hebrews 12:10

I'll never forget the morning our family doctor looked up from a lab report, faced me eyes-on and said, "Your condition is terminal." I felt as though the earth had opened up and swallowed me into an abyss of smothering darkness.

"Give it to me straight, Doc," I managed to say. "I can take it. How much time do I have left?"

"Eighteen months," he replied. "At most two years."

He hesitated a moment, and then added, "Knowing you as I do, Mr. Tam, with your unique religious convictions, I suggest you pray for a heart attack. And soon! This kind of malignancy, as it approaches the final stages, becomes unbearably painful."

In those moments, my mind did not grasp what the Lord was doing. I would have to wait until the day before the operation for that. For the present, I knew that the God I worshiped was not a vengeful God who lurks in the shadows of my life, waiting for an excuse to pounce on me and drag me into His woodshed for punishment.

Rather, I believed—and continue to affirm—that when the Lord afflicts one of His children, His motivation stems from His loving care and kindness!

Every morning, year after year, I had prayed for strength to serve God to my utmost capability. Now, laying on the hospital bed, awaiting surgery the next morning, I anguished as never before.

I began to understand that the Lord had a purpose in what I was experiencing. The Great Physician was underscoring a great truth for me. He was showing me how the route to effective Christian service often involves a price, even a very painful cost.

He also brought to my attention the fact that, as sincere as I thought I was in pursuing God's will, earth-size aspirations still pose a constant threat to me. In fact, I realized, the more determined I would become in placing God's will as priority one, the more diligent and singleminded I would need to be.

God did touch my body and miraculously heal me. I documented the full story in "The Answer," a biographical motion picture and video. I can easily summarize the lesson I learned, however. As I lay despondent on the hospital bed—the pages in my Bible blank, my prayers rising no higher than the ceiling—Stanley Tam's perspective on life changed. I entered the initial stages of understanding God's priorities for me as a Christian.

That experience, now many years past, became to me a personalized parable of the way most Christians select priorities. I can summarize that insight in the words chosen as the title of this book: *God's Woodshed.*

God's Woodshed is not therefore another autobiography. It represents the pathway many Christians follow. And it depicts my heart's prayer that everyone who reads this little volume will be able to identify with me and find relevance for his or her own life.

In fact, my co-author and I make the assumption that we are privileged to have you as a reader not because we have momentous things to say but because your heart hungers, as does ours, for God's very best.

After all, why live in this difficult, dying world unless we want our lives to radiantly reflect the glory of God?

This book, then, will go deeper than merely recounting what I call my "woodshed" experiences. It should help prepare you and others for the disciplines the Lord will bring in order that you, too, might follow Him more effectively.

What do I mean by the concept of a "woodshed"? This term, nearly gone from modern vocabulary, describes a small building usually adjacent to the kitchen entrance of a house. The structure served as a dry storage area for the wood we had prepared as cooking and heating fuel. It also functioned as a discipline center where one's father would apply, as the expression goes, "the board of education to the seat of learning."

I grew up on a 180-acre farm just outside Lima, Ohio. We had 20 acres of timber, and my father and I bucked up many cords a year. In the process, some of the small kindling pieces were set aside as paddles for spankings.

One day, when I was into my early teens, I called Dad "the Old Man." He warned me not to repeat this name. I did, and I experienced a woodshed rendezvous, the painful memory of which I can feel to this day!

I do not begrudge my father for the paddlings he administered. I look on what he did as giving me a "tune-up." He loved us children enough to discipline us for our wrongdoings.

When I speak of "God's woodshed," I perceive of it in similar fashion—as the disciplinary actions of a loving heavenly Father. It's a means by which He permits hurt and heartache to "tune up" His children and confront us with the need to make wrong things right in our lives.

"Your enemy, the devil," the Bible cautions us in First Peter 5:8, "prowls around looking for someone to devour." What a feast he seems to be having these days! Fortunately, there is a remedy: "Submit yourselves, then, to God. Resist the devil and he will flee from you" (James 4:7).

Some people, even Christians, tend to minimize if not ignore the workings of a personal devil. I will give this issue a closer examination in Chapter Three.

I cannot overemphasize, however, the need to recognize Satan's wiles in my determination to live the life of true discipleship, as the following story illustrates.

A friend of mine travels the world on evangelistic projects. He entered Uganda two weeks after Idi Amin fled, talking to scores of believers who had suffered under the mad dictator. He conducted surveys in Eastern Europe, conferring with Christians who had languished for decades under totalitarian governments. He trekked the width and girth of China, analyzing the house church movement and interviewing pastors and laypeople who had languished in prisons and suffered torture and ignominy.

"Today's most persecuted Christians are not in China," he insists. "They didn't suffer under Idi Amin. Nor were they sent to Siberian labor camps. The most persecuted Christians in the world today are in North America. They suffer from Satan's most deceptive and debilitating ruse against consistent, productive discipleship—the anesthetized "persecution" of comfort and affluence!"

Comfort and affluence!

Anesthetized!

May God help me to explain how I and others can live in the family of God and yet be out of the will of God. Occasionally we stray from God without even realizing that such is the case!

I am convinced that churches throng today with Christians who want God to have high priority in their lives but who don't know how to make that happen. Sometimes these people are the kind who seem to be the most impressive. They boast of a good income, the nicest house on the block and two cars in the garage. On the outside, they appear to be brimming with the fullness of life. Inside, however, they are bruised and bleeding from emptiness and unfulfillment.

If you are such a person, take heart!

You may be called upon to spend some time in God's woodshed, but of one thing you can be sure. The weather may be stormy when God puts you through the discipline of spiritual cleansing. But after you emerge from the woodshed, the sun will always be shining!

I know what it's like to listen when the devil insists that happiness is to be found in material abundance. As a young man on the farm, growing up in the limitations of rural economics, I experienced the trauma of being a "have not" who looked longingly into the world of the "haves." The field of dreams for farm kids in those days was a Sears Roebuck catalog. I sat by the hour, looking at the wonder items which could be mine if only I had the money—or if my dad had and was willing!—and could send away for the treasures so appealingly portrayed on those attractive mail-order page layouts.

When, after carefully saving money for many months, I was able to purchase a rusting, wheezy Model-T Ford. I began to experience a taste of how it must feel to be a man of prestige and affluence.

My best friend had an Aunt Nora, who would hurry off to church the moment anybody opened the door. She was convinced young people like me and her nephew Bud were highballing down the road to perdition.

She took it upon herself to bring us into the sober-faced fold of proper church folks. I remember driving down the street in our Ohio town and having Aunt Nora call out from the curb, urging us to turn off the broad way and run full throttle onto the straight and narrow.

This lady may have had the wrong approach, but she had the right idea. The things of this world can be of sizeable hindrance to meaningful Christian discipleship. In my unconverted understanding at the time, I felt sure I was partaking of the very nectar of good fortune. I could be looked upon as Stanley Tam, the clever young man who owned an automobile and drove it with class and distinction.

That's how many people assess God's blessings upon our lives, isn't it? If I have or can buy the things I want, if our health is good, I consider myself the apple of God's eye.

I have attended many midweek prayer services during my three score and more years. I've listened to hundreds of Christians voicing their prayer requests.

Aches and pains.

Those currently in the hospital.

Church members needing jobs or facing other financial uncertainties.

True, Christians should pray for such needs. But the Bible's command to carry each other's burdens, cited in Galatians 6:2 and elsewhere, too often goes no deeper than bank statements and blood pressure diastolics.

What would happen at the average prayer meeting if someone raised his or her hand and said, "I disobeyed God this past week, and I beg you to pray for me"? Or "my heart is so cold, and I know I won't find peace and happiness until the Lord touches me with revival blessing"?

Many midweek groups would sit in stunned silence!

Why?

Because we do not have our priorities straight. We panic when the doctor diagnoses malignancy but remain nonchalant when the Word of God tells us all our righteous acts are like filthy rags (Isaiah 64:6).

My terrifying encounter with cancer taught me that a malignancy of the body is like an afternoon headache compared to cancer of the soul! All over North America, I have met Christians whose lives are impoverished by spiritual disobedience, carnal indifference, unconfessed sins and neglected restitution!

Physical health is a great blessing. I know, for I heard a specialist say, "Mr. Tam, the disease is all over your body."

May God help me to say something significant in this book—that spiritual health is a far greater blessing! This idea burns in my soul like coals of fire waiting to be inscribed upon these pages.

I would rather be on my deathbed, knowing I was right with God, than back in my midlife 40s, brimming with vitality but blighted by spiritual carnality and indifference and disobedience.

Much, much rather!

I urge every reader to hear me out! I do not pose as some malcontent prophet eager to diagnose you as a backslider. Nor will I harangue you with predictions of an impending bankruptcy or a siren-shrieking ambulance trip down the fastest route between your house and the hospital.

I have discovered that God wants His children to be "wealthy" and "healthy," but in a truly spiritual sense.

Indeed, God may bless you with wealth, as He has with me. Very clearly, He has given—as a precious and personal promise to me—the words from His Word that "it is he who gives you the ability to produce wealth" (Deuteronomy 8:18). He doesn't promise the ability to selfishly store up wealth but, rather, he equips the Christian with the skill for transmitting earthly abundance into an eternal, heavenly account.

Our Lima, Ohio, company approaches the $30 million per year mark and continues to grow. We service more than

500 telephone orders daily, plus fax and mail. I detail the secret of our organization in my 160-page book, *God Owns My Business*, of which more than 360,000 copies are in print. We have a record of nearly 3,000 people who came to faith in Christ as a result of reading it!

Praise the Lord!

I thank God for His hand of blessing upon my business, lifting it from almost certain financial collapse to the vitality it enjoys today. But in these pages of *God's Woodshed*, I want to discuss one of the foundations for my partnership with God: His ownership of my body.

"Your body is a temple of the Holy Spirit," says First Corinthians 6:19-20. It is a Christian's most important asset and best potential for profitable investment. "Do not store up for yourselves treasures on earth," the Bible admonishes in Matthew 6:19-20, "but store up for yourselves treasures in heaven." *The Wall Street Journal*, together with every other news and monthly business magazines, cannot possibly offer a more valuable tip on how to get the most out of your cash value and assets!

I know this to be true from many years of experience!

So can you!

God's wealth comes in varying grades of alloy. Some people I meet seem to have the idea God has made me a special case on which to shower His blessings. Quite the contrary! I consider myself a very normal person. I am, in fact, the kind of individual for whom success as a Christian and as a businessman does not come naturally.

I could so easily be numbered with those whom I classify as "handicapped Christians," those who have unconfessed sin blighting their lives the way cancer besieged my body. That's what Satan wants to do, impair us so we will be powerless as Christians.

"Mr. Tam," I've heard others say, "I want to be as you

described in your message, but it's my circumstances—the place where I work, the situation in which I live. If I came clean, I'd be out in the street."

If that's your excuse, let me warn you. This book will major on the experiences of one businessman who somehow had the sense to learn one pivotal lesson: when I am obedient to the Lord, only then can He bless me beyond anything I might otherwise have experienced.

The potential pitfall in modern life involves hiding behind man's laws. Here in Ohio, it is completely legal for me to go down to the tavern near our plant and drink myself drunk. As long as I called my wife to come and drive me home, I would break no state or federal law.

Ah, but what about God's law? This is for me an unlikely—I can even say impossible—circumstance. But there are possibilities, just as pointed, where I could have conducted business within the legalities of man and yet contrary to the law of God.

In my case, abiding by the civil legislation is a vital part of Christian commitment. Naturally, with our volume of business and our special stewardship involvement, the IRS watches us closely. But unless we make an unintentional mistake, which isn't likely with our careful accounting procedures, governmental agents will never find us so much as a dime short on tax payments.

But, as I will describe, Satan has devious tricks for causing me to do wrong at times when, in my complacency, I've told myself that I'm keeping company with Noah, who "was a righteous man, blameless among the people of his time, and he walked with God" (Genesis 6:9).

My wife and I visited a missionary compound in South America, which had a driveway lined with beautiful palm trees. At the top of the entrance road was one tree half the size of the others.

"Did the tree you first planted here die and you replaced it?" I asked.

"No," came the answer. "This stunted tree was planted at the same time as the others."

"Why doesn't it grow?"

"We wondered the same thing, so we invited an agriculturist from the university to come and check it. He found a large rock imbedded in the earth directly underneath the roots. That little tree will never grow like the others."

How similar to secret sin in the life of a Christian!

I told this story at a meeting in Asheville, North Carolina, after which a young lady came to me. She had served at that mission station. "You should see the tree now," she said. "With the agriculturist's guidance, the rock beneath the roots was removed. Also, there was a leak in the water line, which ran directly past the tree, and this leak provided the roots with abundant moisture. Today the tree is taller than all the others!"

Similar "rocks" can also hinder my effectiveness as a Christian!

Let me share an experience I had with a "rock" under the roots of my Christian life, and how God disciplined me in His woodshed until I made things right.

I started out in the silver reclaiming business. This continues to be a small part of our operations. We provide photo processors with a device that collects silver deposits removed from photographic film during one of the stages of development. The concept seems like a contemporary version of the King Midas touch!

During the early years of this venture, however, I nearly went bankrupt. In my despondency, I turned my company over to the Lord. I had times when, being weak and human, I thought I had done God a special favor, and so He owed me blessings unlimited on the basis of such a commitment. I have learned through the years, however, that, as a friend of mine puts it, "Commitment is a lifelong process, in which a Christian learns—by faith—to commit every thought and every act of every moment of every day to the Lord."

In my case, I made available to photo processors a silver collector invented by a man in Cleveland, Ohio. My contract with him stated:

1. I would pay a royalty on every collector sold.
2. I would not question his patent.
3. If I ever quit the silver reclamation business, my customers would become his.

A few years later, a competitor appeared on the scene, using a collector almost identical to the one I had under contract. When I protested, the lawyer told me our patent was so weak there was no way we could successfully wage a contest.

I did some checking and found that he was absolutely right. The Cleveland patent was so inadequate it provided no protection for the inventor's idea and product development.

An obliging demon whispered into my ear. Next morning I went to our attorney.

"If the patent is no good," he said, "neither is the contract. My advice is for you to pay no more royalties." He said he would inform the inventor of this decision.

The inventor sent his attorney to see me.

"The contract is no good," I told him, "and I'll pay no more money."

Legally, I stood on terrain as solid as Gibraltar.

Three years passed. A city-wide evangelistic crusade was scheduled for Lima. A reputable Christian businessman by the name of Stanley Tam, was chosen as prayer chairman.

I felt very honored!

As I knelt in prayer at one of the first group meetings, however, I began to feel uneasy. A pall of guilt came over me. At first I couldn't understand.

Then, eyes closed, I had two distinct mental visualizations—our successful silver collector, and the faces of the inventor and his attorney.

My disturbing sense of guilt intensified!

"Lord," I prayed silently, "I'm doing what our attorney advised and what the inventor's lawyer admitted was my right. I'm within the law 100 percent."

"There are two kinds of laws," a silent voice seemed to tell me. "There is man's and God's, and they are not the same. You are innocent under man's rules. You are guilty under God's law."

I was living a double standard!

For three days, I agonized under a tormented conscience. I would awaken in the night. My appetite waned. When I read my Bible, every verse became an indictment.

God had brought me to His woodshed!

Then I had a luncheon engagement with a prominent Christian friend. Because I was so miserable, I unloaded my heart to him.

Thank God for friends who listen to my heart cry and then give me their honest evaluation. They won't gloss over the situation because they don't want to disturb me.

"Satan has an accusation against you at the throne of God," he said. "I doubt if you will have any power in your life until you correct the wrong you have just shared with me. You know what the Bible says: 'No one should wrong his brother or take advantage of him' (1 Thessalonians 4:6)."

It seems to me that what matters is not whether or not a Christian's conduct is within the limits of the law. Rather, at issue is our relationship with others. Am I exercising the Golden Rule in my conduct?

An important principle was at work. Had I been willing to settle for a run-of-the-pew kind of Christianity, I might have succeeded in quieting my conscience. But I really did have a desire to be an effective Christian, and I was in the first learning stages of what God expects when I declare myself willing to meet His conditions for good spiritual health.

I wrote to the inventor, who then lived on the east coast, and asked for an appointment. "The prodigal son wants to come home," I told him.

I heard immediately from his new lawyer—a friendly man, let me add, who was profoundly impressed by the honesty of someone in the dog-eat-dog world of American commerce.

Isn't God like that, though? Whenever His children set out to meet His conditions, we can always expect opportunities for witness and blessing we would otherwise have missed!

"I'm here on spiritual business," I told the attorney. I briefly gave my testimony. Then I added, "If we can come to a financial arrangement fair to both parties and within my means to pay, you'll find me cooperative."

The agreement wasn't easy. That lawyer, friendly though he may have been, was determined to do his best for his client. But, ultimately, I wasn't negotiating with him. I was dealing with God. And as I wrote R. Stanley Tam on the document the lawyer drew up, a 10-ton weight rolled off my chest!

I walked out of that lawyer's office and headed back to the train station like a new man! My shoes were made of feathers!

On the train, returning to Lima, the Lord rewarded me in the wonderful way He delights to do. He gave me the privilege of leading another passenger to Him!

Two weeks after I signed the new agreement, the inventor suffered a cerebral hemorrhage and died. Then I understood and thanked God for taking me to the woodshed.

God has, since that time, often taken me to task, but I am increasingly grateful for His loving discipline and my increasing determination to obey.

It's the only way to successfully live the Christian life!

WOODCHIPS

Nutshell
Vital Christianity has a price tag: discipline. When we experience discipline, we become involved with our Lord in the closest relationship we can know with Him. God's "woodshed" is synonymous with His grace and goodness.

Branching out
Suggestions for implementing elements of Chapter One into your Christian experience:

1. Read Psalm 139:23-24. Read it once for content.
2. Take a moment to quietly ask God for His guidance.
3. Now read Psalm 139:23-24 again. Read slowly, perhaps several times. Invite the Holy Spirit to penetrate your mind and heart.
4. Write down any specific guidance or reminders which come to mind.
5. Go into action if you wish. Or hold steady as you consider the message of Chapter Two.

2

Who Qualifies for Woodshed Appointments?

Do not love the world or anything in the world. If anyone loves the world, the love of the Father is not in him. 1 John 2:15

Even though I have aspired to be an obedient Christian, as I look back across my life I come to one conclusion. Obedience and discipline go hand-in-hand.

I'm aware of something else, too. Discipline has usually taken place in my experience as a response to a heart-felt desire to glorify God!

For 25 weekends a year, I travel someplace in North America to speak or hold a seminar. In addition, when I'm at home, my telephone rings rather frequently. Thus I talk to a lot of Christians. Many of them tell me how disillusioned they are with the Christian life.

As I chat with such people, I usually find their spiritual experience to be limited to churchgoing, praying and taking quick or infrequent glances at the Bible. All too often I find gross ignorance of the principles of obedience and discipline so clearly spelled out in God's Word.

I've had times of disillusionment, to be sure, but discipline usually occurs for me when my heart yearns for more of God's blessing. It takes place when I tell God that I am a sincere candidate for the purity and power and blessing that the Holy Spirit brings.

In short, this kind of prayer qualifies me for trips to God's woodshed!

I cannot remember enjoying childhood trips to the woodshed to receive disciplinary whippings from my father. He excelled at physical labor and had strong, agile arms. Sometimes, though, my father seemed more loving after he had punished me.

Similarly, God's disciplines always result in blessing. Woodshed encounters provide depths of spiritual experience I never would have known otherwise.

I'd like to describe an all-too-common pre-woodshed situation.

Christian experience, by its very essence, involves interrelationship with other believers. Such Scriptures as Acts 2:42 and First John 1:7 emphasize how God intends members of His family to enjoy fellowship with each other. Problems surface, however, when God's children use the right words but give them the wrong meanings.

This circumstance often arises over the concept of "fellowship."

Someone once said the best definition for fellowship is two fellows in the same ship.

Let me illustrate what the word fellowship means in my vocabulary.

I have had, for over three decades, a prayer partner named Art. Once a week, he and I pull up to a fast food drive-in, pick up a couple of burgers, then head for a quiet park where we spend an hour opening our hearts to each other and to the Lord. The prayers we've seen answered through the years and the enrichment that has come to our lives, would fill the pages of another book.

Such fellowship is priceless!

Men and women are by nature social. Loners are the exception rather than the rule. People I have led to Christ tell me of the fellowship they find in the world.

A bar, for example, often radiates warmth similar to spiritual camaraderie. A young lady, newly converted, says of her father, a bartender, "When I try to witness to him, he tells me he's like the pastor at the church I attend. He listens to peoples' troubles and gives them counsel. He says he's patched up a couple of marriages and helped lots of men and women avoid becoming alcoholics by telling them when to stop drinking for the night and go home. He says he once prevented a man from committing suicide!"

Some Christians experience little more than "alcohol free" friendships. They mistake "friendship" for the "fellowship" described in God's Word. They have folks over after church, or go to a friend's house for coffee and cookies, and enjoy a couple hours of pleasant socializing. No profanity. No dirty stories. In some cases, not even gossip. Instead, sports, business, jokes and chitchat. Nothing is wrong with such social pleasantries, unless we conclude that they represent the essence of Christian fellowship!

It's a good idea for every Christian to take some in-depth personal inventory. How much do you know and experience of genuine fellowship! When did you last sit with another believer and spend 30 minutes talking about your experiences and aspirations as a Christian? Or when did you last call up a friend to discuss concepts in your pastor's Sunday sermon or the key thoughts expressed in your adult Sunday school class or midweek Bible study?

As I see it, in describing today's Christian community, there may well be "fellows" in the same "ship"—or, better, people in the same boat—but, somehow, that vessel keeps rocking! If any one term describes the average congregation today, it would probably be that there's very little smooth sailing. Ask any pastor what most aptly characterizes his counseling and he will likely tell you it's family problems and interpersonal relationships. Jealousy. Bickering. Lost love. Divorce. Children at odds with their parents.

And what about church life itself?

Someone once said that if you want to know how popular a church is, count the people in attendance on Sunday morning. To know how popular the pastor is, count the people in attendance Sunday night. To know how popular the Lord is, count the number of people who come to midweek prayer meeting!

Sunday night?

Prayer meeting?

What church can boast that both of these two events are thriving? Or even existing? Church growth is a big topic these days, and commendably so. But growth in numbers is one thing; growth in spiritual dimensions quite something else!

It seems to me that something or somebody is rocking the boat! Who is the culprit? It's the Christian sitting in the pews, the believer who make it to church most Sunday mornings and never misses on Christmas and Easter. It's those people who, when they get together for so-called fellowship, spend the time in chatting about trivia.

True fellowship, on the other hand, molds believers together so that they exhibit the qualities of Christ, making themselves attractively different from the world!

To the contrary, however, if any one word characterizes most Christians today it's the term "secular."

Anyone can take a simple litmus test to determine how he qualifies as a vital, healthy, productive church member. This test has two elements.

First, such a person exemplifies the Christian characteristics spelled out in the Bible— love, joy, peace, patience, kindness, goodness, faithfulness, gentleness and self-control (Galatians 22-23). How prominent are those characteristics in your daily conduct? When people affront you, or get on your nerves, how many of these characteristics outshine the carnal reactions so typical of human relationships?

It's comparatively simple to act like a Christian, to go through the motions, but it is quite another matter to react like a Christian!

The second litmus test involves your daily, continuing awareness of the terrible truth that, without Christ, every member of your immediate family, every relative, every neighbor, every person in your community, every human being anywhere in the world is a lost soul!

When you meet someone on the street, is your first thought, "Does God want me to speak a word to this person just now?" When a neighbor chats with you about the need for rain on your lawns, does the question run through your mind, "Is there something I can say to help this person realize how eternally important it is to be a Christian?" Do you view your automobile mechanic as somebody who will put your muffler back into shape or, rather, as a person whose heart God may have prepared to hear your sincere and tactful witness!

If someone crosses your path the wrong way, says or does something you find irritating, do you sound off or breathe a silent prayer for guidance? "Lord, is this one of the needing people to whom You want me to reach out this day?"

In short, do you have a continuing 24-hour consciousness that God intends to show His love through you, to speak His message through you, to reach out and touch hurting people through you, your obedience and your initiative?

If you flunk those two tests—as I have many times—but have a heart full of desire to enjoy God's best for your life, then you qualify for God's woodshed!

Don't be frightened! Praise the Lord instead!

I make no claim of being a super or exceptional Christian. Friends ask me what score I shoot in golf or whether I prefer fishing bass or northerns. My answer, as tactfully as I can voice it, is that I own neither golf clubs nor tackle box. Juanita and I do have television programs we watch, when time permits. A well-plotted mystery story holds us both spellbound, and we've become quite adept at sorting out the clues and identifying the villain.

Item one on our agenda, however, is reaching out to people who need the Lord! This is the inevitable result of letting God authenticate the priorities in our lives!

My co-author participates in chapel programs that touch the lives of many professional athletes in North America. Following a session with the Chicago White Sox, he spent several minutes talking to Jeff Torborg, the team manager.

"I kept my Christianity on the back burner during the earlier years of my life in baseball," Jeff said, "but I am determined to make my opportunities in sports also my opportunity to witness."

Our friend Walt Reschlein was a top sales executive with Mobil Oil. He retired to Florida, purchasing a home in one of the more popular golf communities. Four mornings a week, Walt was teeing off. His 18 holes provided good recreation, to be sure, but more importantly, Walt made the links his locale for witness. Many times a foursome retired to the clubhouse for lunch and a continuing discussion of the Christian life.

So golf was not Walt's priority. Witnessing was!

Likewise, I have one foremost priority in my life. God called me to this priority as surely as He calls a preacher to preach or a missionary to head for the regions beyond. It so happens circumstances cause this priority to occur primarily in business relationships—the continuing adventure of leading men and women to a saving knowledge of Jesus Christ!

I'm wary of being labeled "different," however. Shouldn't this kind of Christianity be considered "normal"? What I do is so simple: I carefully search my Bible every day to find out what God wants me to do and what adjustments He wants me to make in my life and conduct. That's not so peculiar! The reason for the unusualness of this lifestyle is, unfortunately, that the majority of God's children have yet to discover how rich and fulfilling life becomes when we obey God and follow the principles spelled out in the Bible.

The Holy Spirit may not lead others as He has led me. The Great Designer, who never fashions two duplicate snowflakes, may not intend an identical course for you. What I am certain of, though, is if you are today little different from your non-Christian neighbors, you can experience transformation which will enrich you beyond anything you can envision.

The life of obedience is the only life worth living!

But if you opt for such a life, you can expect trips to God's woodshed.

So, then, what I have to tell you may not make for easy reading, like a Janette Oke romance or a Bernard Palmer western. But if you'll stay with me, I promise—by God's help—to share with you living concepts and reinforcing experiences that give existence on earth a more attractive hue than you may ever have thought your own life could know.

Some biographical data may help you realize how viable this kind of lifestyle has been for me.

By nature, I tend to be quite shy. I grew up on a farm but, from earliest years, decided I wanted to be a businessman. My first venture, following the purchase of a Model-T Ford, was driving from farm to farm as a door-to-door salesman.

Excruciating at times for a shy guy!

I did make one incredible call where a farmer's wife, obedient to the Holy Spirit's guidance in her life, witnessed to me and sent me on a spiritual search which culminated in my salvation!

Ever since my years in high school, I was determined to be a success. I would scan farm magazines and send away for free samples offered in the ads, looking for a product I could market and thereby launch some kind of private enterprise. Through this search, I learned of the thousands of dollars in silver being washed down laboratory drains simply because nobody was providing a method of salvage.

As I described in Chapter One, I discovered a silver collector and made arrangements to secure and sell it. I worked hard going from town to town as a sales representative. I almost went bankrupt, however, with no small part of the problem being my reticence. A burly lab operator with thunder in his voice would send me on my way in a hurry.

I remember coming home many nights so emotionally upset I turned away from food. To this day, when it comes to human encounters, I tend to prefer corners and shadows to front and center.

Even so—and how I thank God!—the consuming priority of my life is to talk with people, wherever and whenever I meet them, about their need for a personal faith in Jesus Christ. I would much rather sit beside a businessman, showing him from my Bible how he can become a true Christian, than have a 50-yard-line seat at a bowl game.

This dimension in my Christian experience would never have happened without frequent trips to God's woodshed! Because, as I will emphasize throughout God's Woodshed, the more believers ask God for power in the Christian life, the more likely we are to experience the sometimes distressing emotions of divine discipline!

To me, it's a matter of investment. I don't like to waste either time or money. When I give a dollar to God, or when I tell somebody about His love, I am investing in the highest sense. The Bible says, "Do not store up for yourselves treasures on earth...but store up for yourselves treasures in heaven" (Matthew 6:19-20).

People wisely lay up money for a rainy day or for retirement. I happen to believe I can best use my time and possessions by laying them up for eternity!

Some may label me old-fashioned, even legalistic, but I'm every bit as human as everybody else. Sure, my wife and I have television programs we don't like to miss. Sure, I enjoyed romping with our children and now our grandchildren. I'm not too stuffy to play catch with the boys or assemble a jigsaw puzzle with the girls.

If Stanley Tam fulfills, in any way, the description of a disciple of the Lord Jesus, it's not because I am holier-than-thou or endowed with any brand of super spirituality.

To the contrary!

Lest anyone accuse me of preaching, let me use some down-to-earth examples.

Son-in-law Wes and I adhere to a number of very strict principles in business. Between the two of us, we try to stay on top of every detail of operations in our three separate corporations. We delegate, to be sure, but we also keep a hawk's eye on Monday-through-Friday aspects of the total picture.

For years, we've come into our plant Saturday mornings—just the two of us—put on work clothes, taken saws and hammers out of the supply room, and expedited some of the little touches which could be assigned to other staff. We reserve these chores for ourselves so we can keep involved with both the nitty and the gritty at 1390 Neubrecht Road in Lima.

Secondly, we never spend more than we earn. In all my more than 50 years in business, I have borrowed money only once. When we went into an expansive building project awhile back, Juanita and I set aside $600,000. We determined that if we used up that nest egg, the project would remain unfinished until we could afford to proceed.

My wife and I aren't even yet quite sure how it happened, but after we finished the addition—several months ahead of schedule—the building fund balance continued holding steady at $600,000!

For years, I've been intrigued with the life and ministry of George Mueller. A Christian leader during the 1800s, he cared for thousands of orphans in England. Like his contemporary and close friend, Hudson Taylor, he never asked anyone for money. Instead, he told God his needs and asked Him to supply.

On a recent trip to England, Juanita and I sought out the grave of George Mueller. A man, who happened to be in the cemetery, helped us find the site. He was only distantly familiar with the famous Christian. We not only filled him in on the Mueller story but had the privilege of pointing him to faith in the Lord Jesus!

Some may think me presumptuous, but I think people in ministry—such as Hudson Taylor and George Mueller and God's servants today—differ little from the ministry of a Christian layperson who has totally committed his or her business to the Lord.

The body of Christ is a total entity. Speaking of all Christians, the Bible says that "we are God's fellow workers" (1 Corinthians 3:9). In the church, Christ's body here on earth, "there are many parts, but one body. The eye cannot say to the hand, 'I don't need you!' And the head cannot say to the feet, 'I don't need you!' You are the body of Christ, and each one is a part of it" (1 Corinthians 12:20, 21, 27).

This is the concept by which we operate our business. We are in business to make money, to be sure, but money for the Lord's work rather than a fortune for ourselves!

"Not slothful in business" (Romans 12:11, KJV) the Bible admonishes. In other words, to use an expression from the marketplace, give it everything you've got!

In my business.

In my Christian life.

We believe in thorough product advertising. Wes and I invest much money in a simple but attractive catalog that goes to just about everybody who uses plastics products in business or manufacturing. Our computer bank stores every address in the United States!

"Never keep your merchandise and service a secret," is our avowed motto. We emphasize service as much as product. People know that when they dial our toll-free corporate number, they can expect prompt action.

We pay close attention to cost in both the merchandise we manufacture and what we stock from other sources. But we will never sacrifice quality for price. Our customers know we follow strict policies governing quality and mark-ups. We may not be the source of the cheapest price for some items but we strive always to be the best!

And, basic to everything else, we operate on the principle that our business truly belongs to God. I allow myself a modest salary and haven't taken a raise since 1972. The bulk of our profit goes into the Stanita foundation for Christian work across the world.

Our foremost premise in making money—and we try to make lots of it!—is so we will have, each year, thousands more dollars for ministry than we had been able to provide during the previous 12 months.

Of course, we have other policies governing our business but I list these just as examples. It takes good management to run a good business.

My point is that, just as one needs a solid foundation for successful business operations, so one needs good policies for successfully living the Christian life. Yet how many successful Christians can you and I name?

A friend of mine recently traveled to Asia, where he met a missionary who had recently returned from furlough.

"I was a CPA, doing very well financially, when the Lord called my wife and me to overseas ministry," this missionary said. "We had enjoyed our share of affluence. Beautiful home. A car for each of us. Wardrobes. Domestic electronics. Frankly, I marvel that we had sufficient interest in spiritual things so the Lord could catch our attention long enough to challenge us for missions!"

"It was agony," he lamented. "We tried to find one couple our age who really put discipleship at the top of their priorities. We found painfully few. Busy Christians, active in the church, but the best description we've been able to come up with is that they were either sleeping on their oars or rocking the boat. They equated spiritual success with Sunday attendance, large church budgets, even dollars donated for missions."

Does that possibly describe you?

This missionary also said something else. "As we grow older," he told my friend, "we find ourselves evaluating past furloughs. One glaring fact is beginning to haunt us. Each time we return home, Christians seem to identify more with the world than ever before. What they had labeled as worldliness three years earlier was now permissible for 'mature' Christians. Concerns they once had for the church and for their own Christian lives have been put aside or forgotten."

I do believe the church today is full of Christians who yearn to be true disciples of the Lord Jesus Christ. They may be identifying more with the world and less with biblical principles, but they are genuine candidates for God's best in their lives. They long to be involved in the kind of fellowship which calls for more than a cup of coffee and more than chatter about the weather or sports scores.

I also know that those who are failing as Christians are not necessarily bad Christians. In the admonition to love not the world, believers are brought face-on with a very important truth: the status of the world too often becomes the values of God's children. Without even realizing it, the typical Christian finds his thought patterns, and thus his conduct, infiltrated by the surrounding world.

You can change this!

You can rise above mediocrity and complacency and become a Christian who experiences the scriptural premise: "Do not conform any longer to the pattern of this world, but be transformed" (Romans 12:2).

Isn't that what you want? To be transformed? To be a delightfully different person? To have more of God's power in your life? To be close to Him, be loved by Him, someone really special in His sight? The kind of person that can help someone in need?

Then you do, indeed, qualify for woodshed appointments!

Or, more accurately, you qualify for cleansing and transformation in your life!

WOODCHIPS

Nutshell

Committed Christians seem different only because there are so few of them. But spiritual vitality can characterize the life of any believer who sincerely desires it, and who will act upon that longing.

Branching out

Give some thought and prayer to the possibility of implementing some of these suggestions into your life:

1. Think about the "litmus tests" suggested in this chapter.
2. Spend a half hour musing over Galatians 5:22-23, inviting the Holy Spirit to do an inventory of your own life. Take a further look at Psalm 139:23-24.
3. Think, also, about your present activity—or lack of

activity—in personal witnessing.
4. Open your heart to the Holy Spirit's intimate inspection. Be willing to identify anything you need to make right in your Christian life.
5. Thank God for the progress you are making in learning to think, and thus act, like a Christian!

Special assignment:
The next time you are involved in a time of "fellowship," try to exercise some conversational control. Tactfully change the subject from secular topics to your church or, better, something Bible-related. Go easy! Don't push! God will help you!

3

Identify Your Enemy by Name!

The Lord rebuke you, Satan! Zechariah 3:2

How many churches have been perched on the verge of revival, how many lives poised for heaven-sent enrichment, only to settle for desert dust or, at best, a sprinkle of blessing rather than the downpour God intends?

Why does this happen? Because the devil works overtime through the ministry of his fallen angels whom the Bible clearly and frequently identifies as demons.

I want to offer a sobering reflection on the warning, given to Christians in the verse, "Be self-controlled and alert. Your enemy the devil prowls around like a roaring lion looking for someone to devour" (1 Peter 5:8).

When I finally recognized the function of demons, I suddenly became aware of entire new horizons in my Christian life. Like most believers, I had heard missionaries describe witch doctors. I supposed men like Hitler, Hirohito and others who blatantly killed and maimed, to be demon-possessed.

I was also aware of the frequent appearance of demons in the Bible, especially during the on-earth ministry of the Lord

Jesus. I noted, too, that respected leaders like Billy Graham and Warren Wiersbe never hesitated to speak of demons in their preaching and teaching. Further, the more I studied my Bible and learned to relate its message to my life and experience, the more I began to suspect that demons often hoodwink Christians into hiding their sins and disobeying the Holy Spirit's counsel!

In short, I have reached the conclusion that demons are the reason well-intentioned believers become spiritually poverty-stricken!

The next couple of paragraphs may shock many readers, but I firmly believe that more multitudes of demons are in church on any given Sunday morning than were present the night before among the patrons of the bar down the street! The thought of a brothel is ugly, indeed, but demons may be far less active in a den of shame than they are in the pews of a church!

In the tavern and brothel, lost souls have submitted to the wiles of the devil. They give him no contest. By their very natures, they obey his mandates. But in a church, within many Christian communities, inside the life of every reborn Christian, there's a war going on!

Once Satan has failed in keeping you, your Christian friends or your fellow church members from trusting Christ as Savior, he will do his hell-bent heartiest to keep each of you from making Christ the reigning, motivating Lord of your lives!

Satan wages this war against the church—and against individual Christians—through the activity of demons!

What is my basis for such statements? The clear teaching of Ephesians chapter six. Satan has a personal interest in the believer and dispatches his angels to upend my effectiveness and consistency as a Christian.

I find it significant that Ephesians six emphasizes two

major sources of ills in contemporary society—the home and the workplace. Any family which has come to terms with the first four verses of that chapter is a home where happiness reigns. And "masters" and "slaves" in verses five through nine—relevant in those days to the secular world— could as readily be translated "management" and "work force."

In context, then, this chapter shows how a Christian can be fortified against the influence of demons in family life, at work and in personal motivation. It demonstrates how very real demons are and how intently they strive to decimate a Christian's sense of worth. Demons serve Satan in direct opposition to the way angels serve God!

The nonchalance with which some people view the reality of Satan is illustrated in one case I heard about. A man attended a worship service in which the pastor pointed out scriptural references to the existence of Satan. After the sermon, the man said to the pastor, "I'm 60 years old and I've never met this devil you talked about."

The pastor was ready for him and countered, "Maybe you haven't met because you and Satan are both going in the same direction!"

Another important passage on demons is the letter called First John. It's important to remember that this epistle was written primarily to Christians.

"Do not love the world or anything in the world.... For everything in the world—the cravings of sinful man, the lust of his eyes and the boasting of what he has and does—comes not from the Father but from the world. The world and its desires pass away, but the man who does the will of God lives forever" (1 John 2:15-17).

The traditional King James Version uses the terms "lust of the flesh," "lust of the eyes" and "pride of life." Those are the three beachheads the devil attacks, when he declares war against your Christian life.

I believe that the devil prefers to have people think of him as the ogre in the red suit with horns growing out of his head and fire jetting from his nostrils. In actuality, however, the devil often dons a tuxedo and, on most occasions, plain everyday clothes. He strives for respectability. In the case of too many people, Christians included—he succeeds.

In the darkness—the lands of witch doctors and fetishes—Satan desires recognition. In the light—in what we sometimes erroneously classify as advanced cultures—Satan desires obscurity. For example, here in North America, people serve the devil to his delight when they deny his existence!

The phrases "lust of the flesh," lust of the eyes" and "pride" can, of course, pertain to evil in the world. But those three beachheads, as I called them, can just as often, especially for believers, relate to the so-called better things in life.

Even activities at church!

Take a look at "lust of the flesh."

Juanita and I have visited many churches in overseas areas. Even in the hottest of climates, we have never found one with air-conditioning. I'm not criticizing air-conditioned churches per se, but I do suggest that comfortable pews and temperatures could be symptomatic of how the lust of the flesh relates to my life as a Christian. Whenever I enter a luxurious church building, I find myself silently asking, "I wonder how much their missionary budget is?" Could not "lust of the flesh" refer directly to comfort and affluence?

What about the "lust of the eyes" when it comes to the car I drive, the clothes I buy, the money I spend on personal grooming? There's nothing wrong, in right perspective, with any of these things. It's the issue of priorities that I'm addressing.

A Chicago woman liked to host after-church visitors. She would point out the Persian rug on the living room floor, going at length to document the lush under-footing as a dis-

tinct answer to prayer. She had seen it in a Marshall Fields'
window, felt a surge of faith to believe the price would be
marked down to a given figure, and when this happened, she
felt she had no option but to purchase it. Her husband's
salary increased just enough to cover monthly payments on the
Baldwin grand, although the woman herself did not play and
her two daughters scorned music lessons. Much the same
could be said for an answered-prayer refrigerator, a state-of-the-
art dishwasher and sundry other items.

"Isn't the Lord good to us?" she often exclaimed.

But did the Lord undertake in the acquisitions she so
strongly heralded as answers to prayer? Or could it possibly
have been spiritual intervention of another kind? It is not
mine to judge. But I begin to suspect trouble in my life if
I'm giving more priority to things than to the harvest.

I'm careful not to go overboard in the rejection of earth's
good things, however. My challenge as a Christian is to avoid
becoming a starry-eyed mystic who lives in a cardboard-box
house and wears old flour sacks as clothes.

My goal is to learn to live above comfort and affluence,
not without them. As a Christian I need to look and act like a
normal human if I am going to attract non-Christians through
my witness.

In other words, I try to beat the devil at his own game!

In his instructions to Christians at Corinth, the Apostle
Paul warns them to watch out for false teachers. He writes,
"And no wonder, for Satan himself masquerades as an angel of
light!" (2 Corinthians 11:14-15) Then, to his cherished young
friend Timothy, he speaks of "things taught by demons"(1
Timothy 4:1). In the King James Version, the translation is "doctrines that demons teach!"

Satan masquerades as an angel of light!

Demons teach doctrines!

I am not suggesting there might be a pastor in your

community who, when he steps to the pulpit on Sunday morning, is actually a devil in disguise.

Some Bible teachers question whether or not Christians can be demon possessed. To Christians, weak in faith and conduct, the Apostle wrote, "Your body is a temple of the Holy Spirit"(1 Corinthians 6:19). Christ and Satan, these Bible teachers insist, cannot occupy the same temple! It is not my purpose to argue that point.

Speaking to an informal group of leaders one day, Dick Hillis, a well-known missionary statesman, said, "A Christian cannot be demon possessed. I fear, however, that many Christians are demon obsessed. They permit the lust of the flesh, the lust of the eyes and pride to become evil magnets which draw them away from the will of the Lord in their lives."

Demon obsessed!

More concerned about comfort and affluence in the flesh than obedience and fruitfulness in the spirit!

Here, I am convinced, is what the Apostle Paul talked about when he wrote, "Our struggle is not against flesh and blood but against the...powers of this dark world...forces of evil in the heavenly realms"(Ephesians 6:12).

How am I to be victorious over the powers of this dark world? I cannot! In myself, I am doomed to defeat! Just as some unfortunate Christians become proud of their accomplishments in church work, so would be the case with anyone who could claim to have overcome, in his own strength, the wiles of demon obsession.

Just as I can do nothing to merit salvation, but must cast myself completely upon the grace of God, so I cannot live as a victorious Christian apart from the external power available for living my internal life to God's glory.

Illustrating the point of demon obsession, Dick Hillis told of a church elder in pre-Communist China whom God had used mightily in outreach to others. Several new congregations resulted directly from his efforts. At the annual meeting of his denomination, those present named him the senior elder of all their churches. It was a singular honor, never before given.

After returning home, the honored elder's personality began to change. He became critical of others, authoritarian and egotistical. His public prayers sounded more like eloquent speeches than the humble intercession which once characterized his participation in public worship.

One day this elder came to the missionary and launched a tirade of criticism, pointing out weaknesses in the foreigner's Christian life.

"You are a hypocrite!" he shouted. "You should go back to your own country!"

In the silence of his heart, the missionary cried heavenward for wisdom and guidance. "What you say of me may all be true," he told the senior elder, "and I will invite the Holy Spirit to search my heart. But let me share what I suspect of you, my dear brother. I fear that you may be one of God's choice servants who has fallen into the control of a demon."

The elder stood a moment, eyes aflame, lips quivering. Then his attitude changed. Tears came to his eyes. As though smitten, he fell to his knees and cried out, "Yes! Yes! Please help me!"

The next Sunday, this elder stood before the congregation and asked forgiveness. "When I was made the senior elder at our denomination's annual meeting," he said, "a voice seemed to whisper to me. It said, 'At last, the recognition you deserve! Now people will know who is the most spiritual among them.'"

The lust of the flesh and pride! These wiles of the devil function in the very inner circle of church-related Christianity!

How does one avoid falling prey to a similar situation?

As I already cited from James 4:7, "Resist the devil and he will flee from you."

It's as simple as that!

I do not consider myself an exemplary Christian. I have my vulnerable points, my weaknesses. I am merely trying to share how God makes someone strong in weakness. "God chose the weak things of the world to shame the strong" (1 Corinthians 1:27), we are told. I know for sure this pertains to Stanley Tam! For God has shown me that, in admitting my weakness, I qualify for the fortification of His promised strength!

Let me illustrate.

Years ago I began something I can commend to every believer. It takes me 10 minutes to drive from home to the office. During those moments, every morning, I pray aloud. I'm not sure the devil can read our thoughts, so I don't want him to miss a word of my prayers!

"I bind you, Satan," I say, "and command you to leave everything alone at 1390 Neubrecht Road—the property, the building, our Christ is the Answer sign, the conveyors, the high lifts, the computers and the telephones. I demand that you do not cause any employee to lose an order over the phone."

Continuing, I include every detail of our work—the catalogs, the advertising program, each staff person and family, my health, my spirit, everything about me and my family and ministry.

My thoughts frequently turn to the 16th chapter of Ezekiel, verse 16, where the sins of Sodom—pride, gluttony and idleness—are potential perils for Christians of today. Satan is a flagrant secularist. Nothing delights him more than to fill a Christian's life with worldly trivia, even in a religious context, causing indifference, even apathy, toward the real issues of what it means to love and serve the Lord.

That's why I need to rebuke and bind the evil one!

The Holy Spirit may direct other Christians in different ways. The point is to face seriously the teachings in the sixth chapter of Ephesians and, as a child of God, exercise an authority over evil!

The director of a youth camp in New York state once invited me to speak to his young people. As we fellowshiped together, he shared an experience of that summer.

He was in town on business one day and met the camp doctor on the street. He greeted the man, who looked at him but did not return the greeting. This so puzzled the camp director, he turned and retraced his steps to catch up with the doctor.

"Is something wrong?" he asked.

"I realize I'm not your camp doctor anymore," the man said. "I thought I gave you good service and at modest cost."

"But you still are our doctor. We're as pleased as we ever were with your services."

"You have a new doctor."

"No, we don't."

"Now, look," the doctor contended, "my nurse checked our records yesterday. By this time last year, you sent me over 50 sick kids. This year you've only sent three."

"That's because we've only had three campers needing your attention!"

What had happened, this camp director explained to me, was that he had been in a Bible study in which the practice of rebuking and binding Satan was presented and discussed.

Some of the participants protested, saying this practice was done primarily by one theological group. Wisely, however, the teacher pointed out that a daily practice of rebuking Satan is for all Christians.

"We began the practice at camp this year," he told me. "Every morning, by faith, we rebuke and bind Satan and his demons. By our authority as God's children, we forbid evil forces to touch our campers. That, we are convinced, explains the summer health situation with our young people!"

As this story illustrates, could it be that Satan is far more active that the typical Christian realizes? I'm convinced that the answer is yes. By rebuking him, and identifying him as the source of so much havoc in my life, the power of God through me can resist his schemes.

WOODCHIPS

Nutshell
It is possible to ignore or be indifferent to the existence of Satan and thus seem beyond his schemes. In actuality, the Bible tells us his prime target is the Christian. Satan may be functioning most effectively when he seems nowhere near.

Branching out
Dealing with demons is a tough option. You, like so many Christians, may have hang-ups on the subject. But open your mind—and heart!—through a consideration of the following:

1. Read 1 Peter 5:8, 1 John 2:15-17, Ephesians 6:10-17. Also Psalm 24:4-5, Matthew 5:8, 1 Timothy 1:5, 1 Kings 8:61 and 2 Chronicles 19:9. Read the verses several times, slowly, thoughtfully and prayerfully.
2. Invite the Holy Spirit's guidance as to any personal need you sense after considering the verses.
3. Begin each day with this prayer: "Lord, as your born again child, I realize the devil has no right to anything in my life—my body, my mind, my activities. By the authority I have as Your child, I rebuke Satan. I forbid him any right to me this day. I bind him, by faith, and trust You completely for victory in my life!"

4

No Penny Stocks
Available

He who conceals his sins does not prosper, but whoever confesses and renounces them finds mercy. Proverbs 28:13

Juanita, Wes and I are privileged to watch our business, which we've turned over to God, provide for in excess of one million dollars annually for Christian work. This amount could supply considerable resource for Christians who involve their money in stock market transactions. But maybe life on planet earth is not most fully enriched by comfort and affluence as by seeking the greater blessings of spiritual assurance and abundance.

I am a selfish person, as perhaps everyone is, and I want what's best for me. According to God, the ultimate good in this world involves maximizing eternal values and minimizing earth-centered considerations!

My wife and I have traveled to many parts of the Third World—or, more correctly, the Two-Thirds World. We've sat at many a missionary's dinner table with perspiration running down our cheeks. Our sleep has been interrupted by the rest-denying buzz of hungry mosquitoes. And, with most world-traveling Americans, we've experienced a feeling of great relief when our jet touches down in our home country, with its abundant comforts and conveniences.

Sometimes I wonder if believers in other countries and cultures have discovered a dimension of Christian lifestyle that multitudes of Western Christians know little about. Sunday morning services overseas often last from two to four hours. Sermons may be interrupted with a congregational hymn, giving the audience a chance to stretch before the message concludes. If we join a group of believers for after-church fellowship we find, very often, that the subject of conversation centers around concerns and blessings of the Christian life.

Am I asking Western Christians to turn our backs on our technological world? Not at all. The issue at stake is not affluence, but what comes first: my priorities. God doesn't object to my possessions, if He is first in how I obtain and utilize them!

The Christian life is not a system of my deciding what kind of lifestyle I want. Instead, what matters is that I live in direct obedience to the Lord's will.

Obedience!

That's the center and periphery of what the Christian life is all about! By contrast, the pursuit of affluence, simply for the sake of satiating my own fleshly desires, is blatant disobedience!

A Scripture I often reflect on states, "If we confess our sins, he is faithful and just and will forgive us our sins and purify us from all unrighteousness" (1 John 1:9). That message was written primarily to Christians!

Letting myself become swallowed up in comfort and affluence must certainly be labeled as sin. Anything that keeps a Christian from doing what God wants him or her to do is sin. Any action whereby a Christian disobeys God is sin. If I or any other Christian wants God's blessing and guidance, we must deal with the realities of sin.

Sin is at plague proportions among Christians these days.

Often, making things right between ourselves and the Lord becomes a deeply involved and often painful process.

When a believer elects to invest his life and talents for God's glory, he has no easy choices. No penny stocks are available!

In the secular world, most people want power. They want influence. They want to be looked upon as important. I thank God that the greatest thirst He has given me as a Christian is the desire for spiritual power.

No, I don't ask for power so I can exert myself over others. I want power so I can be effective in the great harvest field of helping people find Jesus Christ as their Savior and Lord! I have learned there are no shortcuts to success in the Christian experience.

Having power doesn't mean I am traveling the easy road to spiritual success. When the power of God operates in a Christian, this believer isn't necessarily on a mountaintop. He may be plodding and stumbling through a deep valley.

Through the years my experience has involved a reality which many people find to be new, even startling. The closer one walks with the Lord, the more unclean he or she feels. It's like Isaiah's experience when he came into the Lord's presence. "Woe to me!" Isaiah cried out. "I am a man of unclean lips, and I live among a people of unclean lips" (Isaiah 6:5). Likewise, the Apostle Paul agonized, "I do not understand what I do. For what I want to do I do not do, but what I hate I do" (Romans 7:15).

It's so hard to rid from my mind the erroneous sentiment that walking with the Lord is some kind of blissful and sentimental ego trip!

As the much-loved Psalm 23 affirms, there's some rough geography ahead along the path to victorious living!

Both Isaiah and Paul learned the secret.

Isaiah experienced cleansing and was told, "Your guilt is

taken away and your sin atoned for" (Isaiah 6:7). And the Apostle discovered similar purification. "Who will rescue me from this body of death?" he exclaimed victoriously. "Thanks be to God—through Jesus Christ our Lord!" (Romans 7:24-25). Later, to believers at Corinth, he declared, "Thanks be to God, who always leads us to triumphal procession in Christ." (2 Corinthians 2:14).

As he neared the end of his life, Paul made that dynamic statement, "I have fought the good fight, I have finished the race, I have kept the faith. Now there is in store for me the crown of righteousness" (2 Timothy 4:7-8).

In God's school, success does not come in terms typical of making it big in the world around us. We can learn an important lesson from the oyster. A grain of sand enters its shell and becomes an irritant. Ideally, according to the oyster's point of view, that foreign particle should be spewed out!

In similar fashion, Christians often wish they could be rid of pain and inconveniences in their lives. Instead, as with the oyster, the problem becomes the means of creating something both beautiful and valuable. People pay a lot of money to buy the oyster's problem, because Mr. Mollusk made a pearl out of it!

Believers should assume that the price of spiritual power, of true beauty in the Christian life, is going to involve pain. This could be pain caused in numerous ways including suffering and disappointment. Yet, I have discovered that when someone gets serious about obeying and serving God, this pain inevitably precedes happiness and fulfillment.

Why?

Let me illustrate from experience.

One night, when our children were still at home, I felt overwhelmed with an awareness of debilitating weakness in my Christian life. Things were going well in the business. All our bills were paid. Juanita and I had just purchased a new car and updated some of our kitchen utilities. The children were happy and doing well in school.

Deep in my heart, though, I felt like an empty gourd. I had become a candidate for the kind of spiritual power that comes when I have no strength of my own but reach out in honest desperation for the will of God.

I remember sitting at my desk in spiritual anguish. I would go out, walk around the shop and see all the material blessings God had given me. My heart, with its increasing level of distress, was a different matter.

Most of our staff are believers and so, at times, I felt like calling the workday to a halt and gathering them together to share my concerns.

The matter was too personal for that. It was Stanley Tam "standing in the need of prayer," as the song goes.

Finally one day I looked up from my desk and prayed, "Lord, I've got to get this thing settled! Please help me!" I meant that. Long ago I learned not to pray such a prayer unless I truly was ready for business with God!

I waited that night until my family had retired. At first, as I often do in my alone times, I knelt. Then, in desperation, I sprawled onto the floor.

"God," I prayed, "show me how to have power in my Christian life!"

I knew that trips to God's "woodshed" most often result from my own initiative. That is, when I come dead serious to God, when I tell Him how desperately I want to obey Him, I need to be prepared for discipline! God uses discipline to purify and prepare His children!

Through the years, I've also discovered that when a Christian talks to God, he can expect an answer back! Most often, God speaks through the Bible, His guidebook. Some Christians insist that God has spoken to them in an audible voice. Such has never been the case with me, although God has communicated many times in my thoughts, as clearly—if not more clearly!—than if He had spoken aloud.

As I prayed this night, the Lord said to me: "If you want power, Stanley, you need to do four things. All relate to sins you committed as a young man."

First, after my purchase of a Model-T Ford, I had made a practice of stealing gasoline from my uncle's private pump. When I knew he was gone, such as in town for shopping, I could easily help myself.

Second, being short on cash but wishing to impress my girlfriend, I had cheated on tickets at a student carnival. That had been years before, when I was still in high school, and yet the Lord brought it forcefully to my conscience this night!

Third, again involving the Model-T, I had stolen spare parts from a junk yard dealer and was challenged to confess this wrong.

Fourth, I had attended a country church social where, with a bit of trickery, I was able to help myself to soft drinks without paying for them.

Trivial issues, some might say.

Ah, but that's the crux of it!

The Bible speaks of "the little foxes that ruin the vineyards" (Song of Songs 2:15). The same principle works in a believer's life. Little sins. Wrongs I so easily overlook. But they poison my soul, numb my perceptiveness, my joy in obedience and, most devastating of all, hinder my witness.

"The little foxes...."

My first impulse was to argue with God. These wrongdoings had taken place years before. They seemed so inconsequential. They involved more mischief than wrongdoing. I learned through this experience, however, that it is not for me to decide the measure of my sins!

The Bible says of the Ten Commandments, "Whoever keeps the whole law and yet stumbles at just one point is guilty of breaking all of it" (James 2:10). "All wrongdoing is sin" (1 John 5:17), the Bible further states.

I need to clarify something here. When, through the help of an Ohio farmer's wife, I accepted Jesus Christ as my personal Savior, He changed me from a lost sinner to a child of God. This could happen only through His mercy and grace. The sins I speak about in matters of obedience and discipline have to do with my effectiveness as a Christian. They do not affect salvation.

Tossing and turning on our living room floor, I asked God to give me more power as a Christian. God never gives a haphazard response to such prayers. If I wanted power, I had a price to pay.

Confession and restitution!

"But such tiny things!" I argued. "So long ago!"

I had all but forgotten them.

God still remembered. If I wanted His blessing, then I had to meet His conditions.

Searching the Scriptures, hoping to find some alternative guidance, I came to those words in Ephesians: "We are God's workmanship, created in Christ Jesus to do good works which God prepared in advance for us to do" (Ephesians 2:10).

Why was I created?

"To do good works"!

Not to please myself, or to worry about my own comforts or status or whatever, but to be the channel through whom God does good to others! The good works are not matters of merit, whereby I gain righteousness for myself, but good works are a matter of obedience to my Lord!

Obedience also calls for something else. God created people to do good works because He wants to make something out of us. Left to myself, I may become a good person in my neighbor's eyes. I may be exemplary in my home, at church, in the community. I, left on my own, simply cannot rise to God's standard. By myself I cannot become His workmanship.

God is making the equivalent of computer entries on His children in the data banks of heaven. The Bible says, "We must all appear before the judgment seat of Christ, that each one may receive what is due him for the things done while in the body, whether good or bad" (2 Corinthians 5:10). This has nothing to do with salvation; rather, it is intrinsically linked to our eternal rewards in heaven!

The more I wrestled with this "trivia," as I tried to label it, the more certain I became that any wrong is a major entry in God's computer. I had to make my wrongs right, even though the matter seemed trifling.

Finally I cried out, "I will obey You, Lord! You guide me! You help me! Please, Heavenly Father!"

Immediately, my heart was directed to my uncle. God did that! On my own, I would have left Uncle Glenis until last. He was an unbeliever and would probably attach no spiritual importance to such a small confession. He might even laugh at me and speak to others of my foolish religious notions.

Yet Uncle Glenis was item one on my list!

So I went to see him.

It would have been easier to have stalked unannounced into the office of the governor of Ohio!

My uncle listened in silence, as I stuttered and stammered about stealing from his gasoline supply. I felt miserable and humiliated.

Even as I spoke to Uncle Glenis, the thought crossed my mind that maybe I was doing the wrong thing. My confession would only bolster his criticism of Christians and the phoniness he seemed always to notice in their lives.

"I want to pay you for the gas I took," I said.

"How much did you take?"

"I don't know."

"I'm supposed to know?"

I reached for my billfold. My uncle turned away. Maybe he thought that if I paid him, I would then have license to put him on the spot spiritually and preach to him about his lost soul. Whatever his thoughts, he grunted and walked away.

My confession may have shown little impact upon my uncle, but it made a 20-ton impression on Stanley Tam! A weight lifted from my heart. Joy replaced that weight. It was wonderful!

Even so, as I drove away from my uncle's place, the devil went to work on me.

"Haven't you made a fool of yourself?" the old deceiver seemed to ask. "After seeing how impersonal and unmoved your uncle was, do you really see any sense in doing anything about those other three accusations?"

The devil was a little late making his move, because I had begun a new discovery in my life. At issue was more than a correction of things with my uncle. It was a matter of making things right with the Lord, cleaning up my heart so God could fill it with blessing!

Uncle Glenis, it grieves me say, apparently died without Christ. He lived in another area but I made three subsequent trips to see him. His wife so strongly opposed my coming that I had to see him on the sly. I still remember the look in his eyes as he listened.

I remember, too, my last visit. Aunt Margaret was waiting for me.

"You leave your uncle alone!" she stormed. "He's as good a man as any of your fundamentalist Christians. We have a pastor we can call on if we have questions."

I never talked to my uncle again. As far as I know, he died without receiving Christ as his Savior.

After that first visit with my uncle, I headed immediately for Shawnee High School from which I graduated in 1933. The same superintendent was in charge.

A quagmire of conflicting emotions filled my heart, as I reached the school and headed for the administrative section. I didn't slacken my pace, however. I was determined to do what I knew God wanted me to do.

At the door to the superintendent's suite, I held back a moment. What would I say? How would I begin the conversation? The value of studying the Bible came into crisp definition those moments, as I remembered the experience of Moses when he complained to the Lord about his lack of eloquence.

"Who gave man his mouth?" the Lord had responded to Moses. "Now go; I will help you speak and will teach you what to say" (Exodus 4:11-12).

As I stepped up to the secretary and asked to see the superintendent, she asked, "Have you an appointment?"

An appointment? The thought hadn't crossed my mind!

"It's very important," I managed to say.

"What is the nature of your call?"

"It's personal, very personal."

She looked at me silently for a long moment. The phone rang and she answered it. She obviously thought I would leave.

I didn't.

I must confess, however, that in my heart, I was saying, "I can't talk to the guy if I can't see him, can I, Lord?"

A thought crossed my mind. Maybe this was my Mount Moriah. The Lord wanted to see if I was willing, but would spare me the agony of following through.

I almost left.

After she finished the call, the secretary returned to items on her desk. I tried to make myself head out the door and back to my car. I couldn't. I'm convinced the Lord was giving me staying power, even though I wanted to throw in the sponge.

Several moments later, the secretary looked up at me. Her

eyes caught fire. I turned slightly toward the door.

"Your name?" she asked, as she picked up the telephone with an attitude of disgust.

"Tam," I replied. "I...uh...I graduated here in 1933."

Moments later I was with the superintendent, a man I had almost forgotten since my student days. As I stood there, I had a wonderful experience. I sensed a deep breath of confidence. I discovered that, when God asks someone to do tough things, that's when He moves in and surrounds us with special love and strength!

In addition, the superintendent greeted me warmly.

"It's been years since you were one of our students," he said. "I'm pleased to see you back." He grinned. "Did you forget your notebook? We haven't noticed any misplaced diplomas lying around!"

"I've become a Christian since I was a student here," I said with amazing ease, "and I've come back to make right something I did wrong."

Mr. Lappin leaned forward and rested his elbows on his desk. I'm no expert on body language but I know such posture indicates courtesy and receptiveness. I quickly filled him in on what happened at the school carnival and my desire to make things right in my life.

"This is tremendous, Mr. Tam!" he exclaimed. "What would our world be like if more people had your kind of attitude and commitment?"

I gave a brief witness and, realizing he was busy, offered my hand. I will always remember his firm grip and the glow in his eyes! I learned an additional lesson: When I take the initiative to make things right, I can bring a trove of inspiration and blessing to others.

Next I went to the junk yard. Restitution hadn't been renamed "easy street" by any means, but I felt considerably more poised as I entered the dealer's disarrayed office. He sat at his desk.

"Yeah?" he barked, looking up. He had penetrating eyes. He was a Jewish man with a store of smarts etched deeply across his countenance.

He didn't have a private office, only a desk weaseled in among the dirty motors, drive shafts and sundry car parts. There must have been a half dozen men loitering about the area. They grew quiet, listening. I glanced at them, to indicate that I wished they would leave.

They didn't.

"Need a part for your car?" the dealer prompted.

I shook my head and, with effort, said, "When I was a kid in high school, I stole some things from you."

He rested his right hand on the telephone. For a minute I thought he might call the police! But it was only a mannerism. He put his hand back on his desk.

He waited for me to continue.

I searched for words.

"I had a Model-T Ford," I said. "It was a junker and had a crankshaft with a bearing out of line. I had to replace that bearing as often as once a week."

A couple of the onlookers moved closer.

"I began coming here whenever I needed a part," I continued. "I'd throw the bearing over the fence when nobody was looking, and then leave and pick it up outside. Well, sir, I've become a Christian and I want to make this wrong right."

The dealer once more put his hand on the telephone, again without meaning.

"What was a used bearing worth those days?" he mumbled. "Fifty cents? A quarter?"

"I took about a dozen," I said. "I'd like to repay you."

"I wouldn't know what to bill it under," he quipped. He stood and started to move away.

I offered him a $20 bill. He didn't take it.

"The junkyard wasn't mine at that time," he said. "A widow, Mrs. Golden, owned it. She lives in Louisville now. I'll give you her address."

I sent the money to Mrs. Golden. She gave it to the Red Cross.

Shortly after the junkyard episode, as I was still preparing to act on little fox number four, I received a telephone call from the pastor of the country church I had attended in my youth.

The Lord's timing is incredible!

"We're all intrigued with the way the Lord is using you, Stanley," the pastor said. "People here don't let me forget you were once in our Sunday school and youth group. Our folks are proud of you, and some of them have been suggesting we hold a weekend layman's crusade—Friday night, Saturday and Sunday—with Stanley Tam as the speaker."

"I'd consider it a special privilege," I responded.

I also remembered the fourth wrong—the soft drinks—that I needed to make right! I purposed to take care of that at the meeting.

"Tonight," I began my message on the appointed Friday evening, "I want to speak about God's Woodshed."

"Some of you older people will remember me as Stanley Tam, the farm boy who usually behaved himself reasonably well in church. What you didn't know is that Stanley Tam was like a lot of young people—respectable on the outside but needing the cleansing power of the gospel on the inside."

Then I proceeded to tell about stealing gas, my dishonesty at school and the junkyard pilfering.

The audience sat in total silence. Congregations are usually like that whenever a Christian confesses wrongdoing!

I paused abruptly.

"Is your church treasurer here tonight?" I asked.

An older man raised his hand.

I gestured for him and he came to the front of the church. As we stood there together I told about how I had secretly consumed my fill of soft drinks without paying for them.

"I'm truly sorry for this dishonesty on my part," I said.

Taking a $10 bill from my pocket, I gave it to the treasurer.

"Paid in full?" I asked, my voice choking slightly.

He nodded, tears in his eyes, as he turned and placed the money in one of the offering plates.

God singularly blessed the weekend, with several people receiving Christ into their lives and others making restitution as I had done. To this day, I meet those who date their conversions back to those meetings!

God gave me new boldness in my witness! Those restitutions hadn't been easy, but the aftermath was glorious! I received the power for which I had prayed, seeing more opportunities for witness and more fruit as a result.

"If we confess our sins," the Bible assures us, "God is faithful and just and will forgive us our sins and purify us from all unrighteousness" (1 John 1:9).

How utterly fantastic—made clean!

Purified from all unrighteousness.

Some people have said I am too sensitive about these things. I don't dispute them. I do fear, however, that in many ways the church is becoming too practical—more secular and materialistic. I wonder, as I think about such things, if we might not be stressing "saved by grace" at the expense of emphasizing the need for repentance and restitution.

Repentance and restitution are positive elements in Christian experience. This issue is totally different from a guilt trip! As I search my heart and life, the Holy Spirit may bring to mind sins I have committed openly and against people. These I must confess openly and to people.

There are also intimate sins—attitudes of heart and mind, known only to me and to God—and these I deal with in the intimacy between me and God alone. He does not expect me to stand up in your church and say, "I have been guilty of immoral thoughts, and I want you people to forgive me."

My point is that I must do what the Holy Spirit lays upon my heart. I must implement obedience if I want power in my Christian life!

There is also another factor in this issue of repentance and restitution.

I'm no theologian. My co-author speaks of himself as a "layalogian," a layperson who studies the Bible looking more for guidance in life than to affirm or question some point of doctrine. Theology is important, of course, but "layology" probably best describes my own searching of the Scriptures.

Theology or "layology," you decide, but my co-author and I have discussed whether or not God forgives unconfessed sin. Suppose you die without making right some wrong, even a small wrong, in your life? What happens?

Might it be that such sins come up for decisive consideration at the judgment seat of Christ? "Man is destined to die once," the Bible says, "and after that to face judgment" (Hebrews 9:27). Also, "We must all appear before the judgment seat of Christ, that each one may receive what is due him for the things done while in the body, whether good or bad" (2 Corinthians 5:10). So, then, as I stand before Christ in judgment, my soul saved by His grace, could it be my blessings for eternity might be limited by wrongs I failed to make right during my lifetime?

Whatever the circumstances of future judgment, of this be sure. You will only know the blessings and fulfillment God intends for your here-and-now when you set the record straight with Him and with those with whom you associate here on earth!

Cheap penny stocks are not available for the Christian life in its fullness! But an eternal investment is any Christian's to claim in abundance!

WOODCHIPS

Nutshell

Life for most people is a struggle. For the serious Christian, life is the good fight of faith. Discipline is part of that discipleship.

Branching out

In your continuing desire to experience obedient discipleship, you may find the following helpful:

1. Spend a moment with Job 23:10.
2. Tell God how sincerely you desire quality in your Christian life.
3. Wait quietly for the Holy Spirit to search your heart.
4. Ask God for willingness to follow through on the guidance you sense He is giving you.

5

How to Be Clean
in a Dirty World

If we walk in the light, as he is in the light, we have fellowship with one another, and the blood of Jesus, his Son, purifies us from all sin.
1 John 1:7

"Tomorrow's Sunday," one of my friends heard a factory worker say on a Saturday overtime shift, "and I'd sure like to sleep in. But I've got to go to church and get cleaned up for next week."

That man lived by the theology that governs many a Christian!

As a boy, I experienced once-a-week washups. On Saturday nights at our Ohio farm, Mom brought out the galvanized bath tub, placed it by the kitchen stove and half-filled it with tepid water. Then she brought out the washcloths and scrub brushes. Sometimes, if she gave prolonged attention to an especially dirty spot, I pled for mercy. Time stood still those days during Saturday-night bath time!

When at last allowed to bathe on my own, I remained closely supervised and received tip to toe inspection each time I stepped out of the tub.

"Now, doesn't that feel good, Stanley?" my mother would ask, when an ordeal was finished.

Dutifully, I always nodded my head.

In actuality, though, I had to agree with her. No matter how much I may have disliked those Saturday night baths, it did feel good to be clean!

The reason farm folk settled for Saturday-night clean-ups was a matter of logistics. We didn't have running water, plumbing facilities or sewage drains. Bathing was a production which involved bringing out a special tub we had ordered from Sears Roebuck. It meant heating water on the stove and, after each bath, toting the dirty water outside.

Like the factory worker, too many Christians think of Sunday morning church attendance as a once-a-week clean-up of their spiritual lives. That idea is quite mistaken!

Sometimes when I'm speaking to a dinner group or church, it's difficult to keep tears from my eyes. I look at all those beautiful people and my heart silently cries out, "Lord, how many of them need cleansing?"

How many of God's children fail to realize that being made clean always precedes being made usable?

If you came for a meal at our house, and Juanita placed dirty plates and silverware on the table, how would you respond? I'll tell you what I did in a similar situation.

Traveling in southern Indiana, I stopped at a hotel for the night. Next morning, as I entered the coffee shop for breakfast, I found the place dimly lit. I had almost touched my water glass to my lips when I noticed an ugly bug floating on the liquid. My appetite for breakfast suddenly vanished and I walked out!

Nothing was wrong with the water itself. Similarly, nothing is at fault with the gospel. But an unclean Christian contaminates the message! The world refuses it!

The Bible teaches that "Christ died for our sins." The full

content of that passage affirms that not only did He die for our sins, but "that he was buried, that he was raised on the third day according to the Scriptures" (1 Corinthians 15:3-4). Many people have the idea their sins are completely covered under the blood of the Cross. If we sin, we just tell God and then go on. No need to apologize to anyone or confess open sins publicly or make restitution.

As I said last chapter, I believe Christ died on the cross for sin—singular. That is, for our sinful nature.

But the devil doesn't give up after we're converted. If he cannot damn our souls, he determines to desecrate our lives. He does this through our plural sins. That is, our sinful conduct. God chooses to work through clean lives, and to be clean we must deal with sinful conduct.

What is the greatest sin of misconduct?

The Bible tells us that, in the last days, "people will be lovers of themselves" (2 Timothy 3:2). Pride! Vanity! Selfishness! Openly or blindly worshipping at the altars of the New Age Movement! Are not these heinous sins indeed?

We're all aware how egocentric modern advertising has become. "You deserve a break today." "Aren't you glad you use Dial soap?" "Fulfill your dreams!" "We make this offer just for you!"

Our country seems to be experiencing a heartening return to church attendance. Good! God bless every pastor who sincerely proclaims the life-changing message of the Bible. But I fear too many Christians think Sunday church attendance is all that matters. How they live the Christian life Monday through Saturday isn't so important.

A theologian (or layalogian) can search his Bible for a week, and not find one place where worshiping God is spoken of as a means of cleansing. Purification always took place prior to worship. Old Testament priests carefully bathed themselves before donning their robes and conducting worship

(see Leviticus 16:4). The book of Leviticus abounds with illus-
trations of how defilement was not permitted by anyone entering the temple.

Back then, cleansing was a requirement for worship
rather than the result therof. So it is today, such as with com-
munion, the most sobering of all worship observances (1
Corinthians 11:27).

How to become unsoiled? The only action I can take is to
identify sin in my life, make right what I have done wrong, and
cast myself on the mercy and cleansing power of the Lord!

In fact, if I hope my good works or pious attitudes will
cover for sin in my life, I make my need for cleansing all the
more acute! I am clean when I'm in right standing with God
with my fellow human beings.

Although I am wonderfully blessed with the privilege of
personally bringing people to a saving knowledge of the Lord
Jesus, I consider my primary mission to be outreach to Christians. I want to help create in them the desire to be soul winners! And the most important part of this mission is to guide
people to come clean with God.

No one can be a soul winner without first becoming a
"clean lifer"!

Soul winners must be master controlled by the Holy
Spirit. Eyes, ears, mouth, hands, feet and mind must be controlled by this dynamic power source of heaven itself! Only
then can the will of God be fulfilled in a person's life!

And what is the primary will of God? Bringing people to
the Lord!

"He is patient with you, not wanting anyone to perish" (2
Peter 3:9).

How then do I best fit into the will of God? By winning
souls!

"He who wins souls is wise" (Proverbs 11:30).

Thus, in anything I do—run a business, work in a factory,

direct a choir, look after a home—my first and ultimate concern is for people to find salvation through my witness and deed!

For this to happen, God needs clean vessels of service!

But even as I disliked those Saturday-night baths on the farm, so we Christians often don't like to pay the price of becoming undefiled.

As I've said, the biggest obstacle is pride. Everyone seems to get wrapped up in the question, "What will others think?" Even Christians tend to be "lovers of ourselves."

It isn't easy to tell someone you've done wrong and to ask forgiveness. As Charles Finney, one of the greatest influences in my life, powerfully observed: "You cannot experience revival without Christians confessing their sins."

A Christian can experience peace and fulfillment only by being sure his heart, mind and conscience are free of unconfessed sin.

Most everyone has watched a detergent advertisement about a so-called Mr. Clean. I, for one, do not want a title of "Mr. Clean Christian." Stanley Tam is simply a hell-deserving sinner saved by the blood of Christ and cleansed by the Holy Spirit's application of Scripture to his life. Any effort made to "clean up my act," as some would put it, would serve only to deepen my awareness of guilt.

Cleanliness must take place God's way, the Bible way!

I've met Christians who let themselves be led onto guilt trips. They become spiritual hypochondriacs. Their behavior can be one of the devil's tricks to keep such believers from enjoying the peace and forgiveness and cleansing to which they are entitled (Revelation 12:9).

This factor also explains why, as I commented earlier, I begin every day rebuking Satan. There are times when the great deceiver attacks my conscience. If the phone rings, and a businessman who has been touched by our book and video ministry asks for information, I must be sure my life is clean before I talk to him. The devil knows this, of course!

Another of Satan's favorite ploys is to bring up old garbage, something you have confessed and made right.

When this happens, I can rebuke him! It's my right as a child of God!

"Sin shall not be your master, because you are not under law, but under grace" (Romans 6:14).

Finally, it's probably impossible to remember, much less make right, all wrongs done in my life. So I must take care not to let the devil lead me into a self-persecuting guilt trip. What's at stake here is obedience.

This is not to say the Holy Spirit will remind me only of big things. He may bring to mind some seemingly insignificant sins. That's what He did for me, as I described in Chapter Four "the foxes, the little foxes that ruin the vineyards" (Song of Songs 2:15).

In fact, a very important truth to keep in mind is that often the sin separating me from victorious living may be only a small sin.

Let me illustrate.

One Sunday night in the middle of winter, my wife and I returned from church to a cold house.

"Why do these things always happen on weekends," Juanita lamented, "when repairmen don't like to be bothered?"

I called our furnace technician, apologizing for my request that he come as quickly as possible. Juanita had already wrapped herself in a blanket, as she prepared hot coffee, and I had my collar turned up against the chill.

"It may not be necessary for me to come," the man said. "Go to your thermostat. You will find two electric contact points. Maybe dust has gathered and broken the contacts. Take a piece of paper and pull it through those points. It's simple and may do the trick."

It seemed far too easy, and I thought the man was putting me off. But I did what he said. As I pulled the paper through those electric contacts, I heard a click.

"The furnace just went on!" Juanita called out.

Moments later, a flow of warm air came up through the registers.

This is what happens in the Christian life, when I keep the contact clean between me and the Holy Spirit.

A Sunday school teacher once asked her class of youngsters why it was so easy to do wrong and so hard to do right. In response, one child replied, "I guess it's because we were all born crooked."

I think, as that Sunday school scholar indicated, people are the same as they have always been. As the Apostle Paul said it, "What I want to do I do not do, but what I hate I do" (Romans 7:15). The difference today is that sin has become so socially acceptable.

The world today is seething with sin! When I was a child, anyone who lived in open sin was considered an oddity. By contrast, today it seems that someone adhering to righteousness is the odd ball!

What I really fear, in this matter of cleanliness, is the fact that so many Christians today hold membership in what I call The Twenty-Five Percent Club. They are involved in so many things they give God only one-fourth of their time. They seem to have succumbed to the New Age Movement in that they allow themselves to sit on the throne of their lives.

Often without knowing it, they play God and make the crucial decisions. They permit pleasure and self-gratification to take the place of God's peace and fulfillment. The result, as I heard one speaker say, "If Christ isn't Lord of all in your life, perhaps He isn't Lord at all!"

In the early days of my Christian life, I had an experience similar to what happened with those dirty contact points on our thermostat. Whenever I prayed, I began to see a pair of gloves. I tried to shake this from my mind, because it was something from my past.

I'm glad I was sensitive to this prompting of the Holy Spirit, because I have learned that unwillingness to put sin aside—even a small sin from the distant past—can be as wrong in God's eyes as the sin itself!

In my case, the Holy Spirit was bringing to my mind an time, two years prior to my conversion, when I walked into a J. C. Penny store and saw a pair of gloves I liked. The clerk was looking the other way. There were no customers in the area. So I took the gloves, wore them to shreds and forgot about them.

Until after my conversion!

When the gloves came to mind, I would shrug my shoulders and remind the Lord how long it had been. Weren't all my sins settled when I knelt at that church altar and invited the Lord Jesus into my heart?

True, at that church altar, God had dealt with how my sinful nature affected my eternal destiny. Now, however, I had to deal with the sins of conduct that were still part of my new Christian life. I had become a new person in Christ as a result of my conversion. This transformation explained why the Holy Spirit brought to mind the gloves I stole from the J. C. Penny store.

One Sunday our pastor preached a sermon on restitution. Right there in the pew, a shy young Christian silently prayed, "Lord, it scares me to think about it, but if You'll give me the courage, I'll make this thing right."

It was hard to pray such a prayer. But next day, as I hesitated outside Lima's J. C. Penny store, I had to grapple with something even more difficult: the potentiality of a trip to jail!

As the devil will do in times like this, he went to work on my natural shyness and tried to convince me that the store manager would only laugh at me. A pair of gloves? Under eight dollars? And so long ago?

I might have turned away, but the pastor's sermon came to my mind as clearly as if he were by my side repeating it to me!

"Give me courage, Lord," I whispered.

He did. I took a deep breath, walked through the door and asked the first clerk I saw how I could find the manager's office.

"We aren't hiring," the clerk said, probably worried about his own job.

"I'm not applying," I countered.

"Mr. Zuber's office is on the third floor."

Again, panic and shyness came over me. But I had made the first step. I've learned that, when someone takes the first step, the Holy Spirit helps with the rest of them!

"What can I do for you, son?" Mr. Zuber asked. He smiled. His pleasant attitude helped me to proceed.

"I've become a Christian," I blurted, "and three years ago I stole a pair of gloves from your store."

I told him how I thought I had forgotten the incident. I told him how our pastor's sermon reawakened my conscience.

Mr. Zuber put his arm across my shoulders and, tender as a loving parent, said, "I know some of the people who attend your church. Like many of them, you have demonstrated true Christianity this morning. Your honesty is payment enough."

"But I'd feel better if I could make everything fully right," I said, as I took out eight dollar bills and pressed them into his hand.

When I left the J. C. Penny store that morning, I felt cleaner than a kid after a Saturday-night bath! Revival surged in my heart. Revival, I was beginning to learn, is a fresh return, through obedience, to the leading of the Holy Spirit in our lives.

You may not have serious wrongs needing to be made

right. You may need attitude changes. Or maybe cleansing from all the trivia involved in your use of time. Or perhaps any of many other shortcomings the Holy Spirit will point out to you.

For example, we receive well over 1,000 telephone calls per day from customers ordering our products. These phone calls result from the catalogs we mail out 12 times a year to tens of thousands of active and potential customers. Thus we are very aware of the need to "clean up the mailing list" as people in direct mail put it.

Duplicate names and wrong addresses can pose a major problem to direct-mail people.

So we recently installed a marvelous new computer. It stores every street address in the United States and is updated for us by the post office. When we address mailing labels, this computer will not permit us to mail duplicate copies to the same person. One wrong address costs us more than $10 a year. Needless to say, our computer quickly paid for itself!

How then do we live clean in a dirty world?

Basically, we follow the same process we follow for bodily cleanliness. Instead of a once-a-week bath, we ask the Lord for daily cleansing. The results produce moment-by-moment alertness to the wiles of the devil. We also become engaged in the kind of interpersonal relationships which involve fellowship more than mere friendship!

Walking with God can be a practical experience!

Try it!

WOODCHIPS

Nutshell

Living clean as a Christian involves making work of being a genuinely holy person. The experience is one of daily washing. It calls for letting the Holy Spirit inspect you from tip to toe for any "dirt" that is awaiting repentance and restitution.

Branching out

Here are some thoughts on being made and kept clean:

1. Look up these Bible verses, taking a few moments to let each infiltrate your mind and heart. Job 14:4; Isaiah 1:18; Ezekiel 36:25-27; Psalm 51:10.

2. Invite the Holy Spirit to point out any need for cleansing in your life.

3. Determine to follow the Holy Spirit's guidance in every detail.

6

Doing Wrong
Is Never Right

So whether you eat or drink or whatever you do, do it all for the glory of God. 1 Corinthians 10:31

In recent decades, certain theologians proposed the theory that Christians may face circumstances in which it is right to do wrong. They called this value system situation ethics.

For example, a friend of mine rushed to the bedside of his father.

"He won't live until sundown," said the doctor, "but don't tell him that. If he asks, tell him I said his condition has improved since yesterday."

Fortunately, the dying man was a believer. After his death, however, a situation surfaced in which another member of the family brought a strong accusation against the deceased.

"I can't be sure," my friend says, "but it seemed my father wanted to tell me something. Yet, from circumstances at the time, he seemed quite unaware that death was so imminent."

Did the grieving son do wrong by not telling his father the physician said he would die before sundown?

I realize the doctor had good intentions, not wishing to

disturb the patient. I realize, also, that the theologians had in mind circumstances where—in their opinion, not mine— untruth would be more loving than honesty.

I want to investigate certain situations in which a Christian may think it right to do wrong, where circumstances occur that could be interpreted as a kindness or directive sent from heaven.

In actuality, doing wrong must never be excused as doing right. If I want the Holy Spirit's cleansing and blessing in my life, I dare not play games with basic integrity and principles!

First, let me outline some of my basic convictions:

1. This is an age of permissiveness. Wrong is right, in the opinion of this world, as long as it helps "me" without hurting anyone else.
2. The forces of evil are arrayed against Christians and the church in all-out effort, as predicted in the Bible, before the return of Christ.
3. Only one Christian in 60 ever makes an effort to help another person experience personal salvation.
4. Little sins, more than big sins, hinder a Christian's growth and spiritual power.

After I had addressed students at a southern Illinois college, a young lady came to the platform to speak with me. She told me she needed glasses but was hindered by a very limited budget. "I asked God either to heal my eyes or to provide the money I needed," she said.

"God didn't heal my eyes. Instead, they got progressively worse. I knew I needed glasses."

She made an appointment with a local optometrist, quite distressed over a cost she knew she couldn't afford.

"He quoted for me the cost of the examination and the cost of the glasses," she said. "I asked for the least expensive glasses possible. Even so, the total amount would severely strain my budget. I made it a matter of urgent prayer."

When she received the bill, she was pleased to see that she had been charged only for the glasses, not for the examination. Her first thought was that the doctor had shown mercy!

Was that a situation of answered prayer or a test of this young lady's Christian integrity? She had hoped it would be the former!

Then she heard me speak. My text had been, "Whoever can be trusted with very little can also be trusted with much, and whoever is dishonest with very little will also be dishonest with much" (Luke 16:10).

In response, she went to the optometrist's office and learned that the lady in charge of billing had made a mistake. She paid the extra amount, out of money she had eked from her budget for personal things, and experienced release from guilt and a new sense of God's presence and blessing in her life.

In silver refining, our company can only process high content reclamations. Sometimes we get material which would require such a long firing it would be unprofitable for us. We collect this kind of stock and send it to a larger silver refinery in Chicago. They wait until they have accumulated 20 tons, which they put into their big furnace to cook for about three weeks.

We sent them a ton of material and received a check for $5,000—twice as much as we knew it was worth.

These apparent windfalls occur for a lot of businesses and individuals. For the Christian merchant, do I interpret it as an extra benefit or do I make it right?

I receive only a modest salary. I haven't given myself a raise in more than 20 years. Why not give $2,000 to the Lord and keep $1,000 to spend on a forthcoming overseas missionary trip my wife and I were about to make? More than enough carnality resides in my heart to do such a thing!

I wrote to the refinery and asked them to reassess the

billing. The proprietor sent me a curt letter, thinking I wanted to squeeze him for a few extra dollars. I insisted, not giving my reason. Reluctantly, they complied and found they had paid us $3,000 more than the actual value of our material.

I promptly sent a refund check in this amount.

On a subsequent trip to Chicago, I stopped by this plant, as I frequently do, and was invited out to dinner with two employees—two non-churchgoers and the Jewish boss.

After we ordered our meal, the boss turned to me and said, "Tell us, Mr. Tam, what it means when you say God is your senior partner."

"Do you want the whole story?" I asked.

"Yes!" he said. "The food is good here but service is a little slow."

I told how I was converted, how I almost went bankrupt and how God blessed our business after my wife and I turned it over to Him.

It took 30 minutes, but my small audience didn't take their eyes off me.

"Did that Jewish man believe you?" I've had people ask. To which I reply, "When you refund $3,000 to someone, he believes you!"

When Billy Sunday was a young man, prior to his career in professional baseball and as a famous evangelist, he became involved in a banking error which netted him an unexpected $15. In those days, that was more than his income for a week. A person could purchase a new car for less than $1,000 and a middle class house for under $3,000!

Although not yet converted, Billy was honest and felt he should return the money.

He asked advice from a businessman of high reputation in the community.

"Hasn't the bank asked you about the $15 overage, Billy?"

"No, sir."

The businessman laughed heartily. "Then keep the money! It would serve that bank right for all the times it has taken the skin off somebody else's nose!"

Billy bought a new suit of clothes, made of cloth much finer than his limited salary would normally allow him to purchase.

"How did you afford that outfit, Billy?" his friends wanted know. "Did a rich uncle leave you some money?"

The bank never discovered the error. But Billy Sunday lived for years with the knowledge of his guilt. After his conversion, he made a special trip to the bank and paid back the $15 plus accumulated interest!

When he preached sermons on repentance and restitution, he often related that experience. "Ah, friend," he would exclaim, "it feels so good to be clean! Let God make you clean tonight!"

Following one of my weekend seminars, a well-dressed and rather distinguished gentleman came to me.

"You've heard the saying," he began, "there's no such thing as an honest car dealer." He was trying to be nonchalant but I knew something was bothering him. "Weren't you a little hard on us tonight?"

"How do you mean?" I asked.

"Well, look," he continued, "in my line of work—honestly, Mr. Tam—I'd be out of business if I hewed as close to the line as you talked about tonight."

"I'm not out of business," I replied.

I'll always remember the hurt and hungering look in his eyes as he turned and walked away.

If only I could have helped him understand that honesty is not a hindrance to success in business. Rather, integrity is a valuable aid to success in business. But, more importantly, honesty is an absolute prerequisite to success as a Christian!

In addition, when a Christian is dishonest, that person

usually carries a hidden load of guilt which functions like a debilitating disease. Repentance and restitution alone can lift the burden. The resulting peace and happiness make an obedient Christian wonder how he or she ever allowed the misery and spiritual powerlessness to persist for so long!

A man came to my hotel one Sunday morning.

"I haven't slept since I heard you speak last night," he told me. "If I make things right the way you told us to do, I can expect 10 years in prison. Maybe more."

He glanced nervously over his shoulder, fearful lest someone be listening.

"We're alone," I assured him. "Nobody's listening except you, me and the Lord. What's your problem?"

"A few years ago," he began, "I had a partner in the trucking business. Our work was touch and go all the time. When it looked like we might make a little extra profit, we'd get hung with a repair bill. Or something we'd be depending on would fall through.

"One day I was driving and went into the ditch, stuck pretty badly. It was on a little-used road and I had to walk a mile to call my partner. He told me he'd be right out with a wrecker. Instead, he came in his car.

"He looked at the truck and said, 'We need cash more than we need this old heap.' So, while I watched, he unscrewed the gas cap and tossed in a match. The truck was ablaze in seconds.

"Immediately, the ethics of what he'd done bothered me, but my partner said he'd take care of it. He did, and without a hitch the insurance company paid us $20,000."

Tears came to his eyes. I laid my hand on his arm, trying to encourage him.

"Shortly after that, we dissolved our partnership. But I'm a Christian. I know we did wrong. The more time passes, the more it bothers me."

He hesitated. I waited. "The catch is that, if I come clean with the insurance company, it'll hurt my former partner as well as put me behind bars."

"Do what you know is right," I told him, "and the Lord will stand by you, even if it means doing time."

He stood silent for a long moment.

"May I pray for you?" I asked.

He nodded.

I prayed, asking God to encourage him, to help him do what he knew he must. After my "amen," he stood another moment. He tried to speak but couldn't. Impulsively, he turned and hurried away.

During those next days, I prayed much for this man. I prayed he might discover, as I had so many times, what blessing can await those who tough it out through a woodshed ordeal.

One day I received a letter.

"I struggled another week," he wrote. "As you warned me, the devil filled my mind with excuses. But I finally went to the insurance company, told them exactly what had happened. I told them I am a Christian and that was why I was doing what I was doing. They said they would bring up the matter to their board and be back in touch with me.

"You know, Mr. Tam, as I waited for the decision, something wonderful happened: God filled my heart with peace! Come prison or whatever, I knew I had done right. I understood the value of being honest."

The insurance company board was so impressed by the man's honesty that they sent him a letter absolving him of any guilt!

Wrong is wrong, no matter how someone colors it. The only way to have peace and power in life is to make the wrong right. I must deal privately with the Lord, if it's a matter between Him and me, or go public as in the case of the trucking business partner.

This principle works even in cases when we might tend to overlook restitution.

One Christmas, our family went to Rockford, Illinois, to be with my wife's relatives. Rockford is a Scandinavian town where they know how to make Christmas festive with a smorgasbord of lutefisk, meat balls, potatiskorv, ostkaka, limpa bread, lingon berries and all the trimmings.

It was a happy time.

God had been good to us in the business, and I was increasingly grateful. I sensed His blessing in a special way.

"You know, honey," I said to Juanita, "I'd like to finish the year absolutely sure everything is right between me and the Lord."

So, after everyone else retired, I remained down in the living room. I turned the lights low and got down on my knees.

"Lord," I prayed quietly but aloud, "take inventory of my life tonight. Is there anything I've done or am doing contrary to Your will?"

Immediately this statement came to mind: "You have $4,000 that doesn't belong to you."

During the previous week, our accountant had come to my office.

"I'm closing the books for the year," he said, "and I can't get our silver purchases and sales to balance. The silver that's come in from collectors must have been 95 percent pure but we paid commissions only on 94 percent."

"How much does that come to?" I had asked.

"Four thousand dollars," our accountant had replied. He chuckled. "We've got 3,000 customers, so it's hardly anything to think about, is it?"

"I suppose not," I remembered replying.

He suggested how he could make an entry to bring the accounts into balance, and I let it go at that, not giving the disparity a second thought until I knelt in my in-laws' living room there in Rockford!

"Lord," I continued my prayer, "that would average $1.30 per customer. Not one of them would expect that level of reimbursement."

"Four thousand dollars that do not belong to you!" The thought stayed with me.

I had been a Christian long enough to know that when the Holy Spirit speaks, I have two options.

The first is obedience.

The second is disobedience, tantamount to pulling the switch and shutting off spiritual power in my life.

I knelt quietly a moment. Perhaps God was asking only for my willingness.

"Four thousand dollars!"

"All right, Lord!" I retorted. "I'll do it!"

When I told Juanita the next morning, she looked at me for a long moment. Then she said, "Whatever the Lord tells you to do, sweetheart, be sure to do it! Small wrongs are the same size to God as big ones!"

That's the kind of wife Juanita is!

We hired a woman to work full-time on the project.

"Here's a refund of only 12 cents," she told me one morning. "Do we issue a check?"

"Make the payment in postage stamps," I replied.

At that time, 12 cents in postage would send two first-class letters!

As she left my office, this part-time girl commented, "Looks like the largest payment will be $17."

When we were about to take the 3,000 letters to the post office, the Lord again spoke to me.

"Stanley, aren't you going to tell your customers why you're making the refund?"

"But the refunds are so small, Lord," I countered. "Even the largest of them. Those customers would laugh at me.

Wouldn't it hurt my testimony?"

But the thought persisted.

And, from experience, I knew better than to disobey!

So I prepared a special form letter, explaining that we were making the refund because God owned our business and we were doing what we felt sure He wanted us to do.

We put a printed copy of my testimony in each envelope.

"We'll not hear from anybody," I predicted to Juanita, "because of the testimony."

"Will customers think you're foolish?" she asked.

"Some will," I said. "Maybe many of them."

I silently cringed. I don't like ridicule. It wouldn't have taken much persuasion for me to cancel the mailing and dump all those envelopes into the trash.

"But if you're doing what you know the Lord wants you to do...." My wife's voice trailed off into silence.

So off to the post office went the letters.

We were not prepared for what happened.

Hundreds of responses came flooding back to our mailbox. Amazed and satisfied customers reacted to what we had done, many of whom had never sent us any communication other than an order blank or a paid invoice!

"We'd been looking around for a better outlet to sell our silver, but we're sticking with you people."

"It's satisfying to know our silver goes to a company with your kind of integrity."

"We sometimes question, in this day and age, if our shipments might be assayed a few ounces short. We won't wonder anymore!"

"We've talked about your religion angle, those little pamphlets enclosed with every shipment. We'd never before grasped what you were driving at. Now we understand."

"I am a Roman Catholic sister and we send you the silver

from our hospital x-rays. Frankly, we haven't been as much interested in the earnings as in those tracts you enclose. Each one seems to speak to our hearts in a new way. Wouldn't it be wonderful if all businesses were conducted the way you manage yours?"

My wife and I were in awe at what the Lord had done! We wept as we read the letters.

"How does that Bible verse go?" Juanita asked one morning at breakfast. " 'To obey is better than sacrifice,' (1 Samuel 15:22). I used to hear the verse in Sunday school and wonder what it meant." She sipped her coffee for a reflective moment. Then she said, "Thanks for obeying the Lord, Stanley!"

I'm not one given to outward displays of emotion. But my heart surged with praise and gratitude to the Lord. I learned, as my wife so aptly put it, big or little are all the same size in God's measurements. Also, even a small act of obedience can provide an overflow of blessing. As one modern advertisement affirms, "You can't beat the experience!"

Over and over, following that refund adventure, I have prayed, "Lord, guide me to show people what it can mean to obey Your Word and the promptings of the Holy Spirit!"

Quite opposite to our predictions, the $4,000 turned out to be the most productive advertising dollars we ever invested! Within four months, we received that amount back in new business! Best of all, this small Christian gesture helped boost our company image immensely.

I went down to our local camera shop to pick up some film. The manager came out from the back and handed me the check we had sent him. For a moment I thought this might be the first protest we would receive.

"Here's the seven bucks you sent us, Mr. Tam," the manager said.

"But it belongs to you," I told him.

"I think it belongs to God! I'd like you to add it to all that money you give to religious work around the world!"

At that time we had a research project underway at Michigan State University which I dropped in occasionally to check. On my next trip to East Lansing, I happened to see a camera shop I hadn't noticed before and decided to show them our silver collector.

"Nothin' new about this," the owner told me. "We read in a magazine we get about a company in Ohio that supplies these things. But we haven't got around to doing it yet."

"What's the name of this company?" I asked.

"Can't remember the name," he answered, "but it's run by some guy who claims God is his senior partner. I was at a convention last week, and all the photographers were talking about how this Ohio fellow gave a special refund to customers he'd underpaid."

I took out my New Testament.

"That's my company they told you about," I said. "Here are my credentials."

The man glanced at the New Testament. He looked up at me. He gazed back at the Testament.

"The usual businessman doesn't carry a Bible around with him!" the man said.

I left a silver collector at that shop, then went to a customer we had for several years. The proprietor of this second store was a profane unbeliever. More than once during previous visits he had cursed at me for mixing religion with business.

When I called on him that day, however, he was as meek as a well-mannered boy in Sunday school.

"We got your 13 dollar check," he greeted me. "I showed it to our lab man and he said it must be a mistake. He hadn't sent in any ripe silver collectors in two or three months. Then we saw what it was for. Now don't push me, Mr. Tam. But I'll tell you something. You've got us convinced religion really does make a difference in your business. We won't throw those pamphlets away anymore. We've all decided to read them!"

Big blessing from small obedience!

I could fill a chapter with examples of how God blessed us, and blessed hundreds of our customers, through those refund letters. Instead I'll describe just one instance involving a man named Ed Haas. His story not only ranks at the top of refund check-blessings but, actually, at the top of the many ways God has touched our ministry and our efforts to obey Him.

Ed was one of our customers in Stamford, Connecticut, mailing in silver collectors for us to melt down, assay and then remunerate him. Unfortunately, he went out of business, and we lost track of him.

We did but God didn't!

Ed knew nothing about the refund checks when he rummaged through some old papers and found our address. He decided to write and tell me he was now a salesman for a photographic supply house in New York City.

"I travel around a bit," he wrote, "and could market those silver collectors I used in my own business three years ago. You would pay me a commission instead of a salary. If I produce, I earn. If I don't produce, I cost you nothing."

We signed him up!

Ed did so well that he wrote and asked if he could work full-time for us on salary plus commission. I invited him to come out for a visit. I met him at the train station. He was in his early 40s, was Jewish and radiated a warm and engaging personality. I hired him before the day was over.

"You've been setting up new customers," I told him, "many of whom will have questions about the silver collector. Since you used the collectors yourself for several years you can maybe troubleshoot for us."

"Sure can," he agreed.

So Ed began servicing the new clients he had set up for us. Also, when he went through a town where we had an established user, he stopped in to see them.

"I'm from States Smelting and Refining in Lima, Ohio," he introduced himself, as he called on the first such firm.

"Oh yeah, sure!" the proprietor interrupted. "The religious people!"

Well, uh—," Ed stammered.

Before he could say anything the man darted back to his office and came out with his copy of my testimony.

"Here is this pamphlet you people sent us," he said. "We've been discussing it and trying to figure it out. What does Mr. Tam mean when he talks about being 'born again'?

"Born a-what?" Ed asked. He took the pamphlet for closer inspection. The proprietor had circled the words and pointed them out.

"We reckon it's got something to do with Christianity."

"Yeah," Ed said, sucking air through his teeth, "I 'spect it does."

In reality it was the first time Ed Haas had encountered those words!

"I'll be checking in with Mr. Tam tomorrow," he responded, "and I'll ask him. Then I'll stop by and tell you what he says."

This scenario happened repeatedly for Ed!

Customers wanted to know about the Bible's message, expressions like "saving faith" and how humans could actually talk to God through prayer and get answers back.

Ed wrote down the questions, referred them to his boss and brought the answers back to his customers.

"Sounds a little like voodoo or something," one man snarled.

It wasn't voodoo to Ed Haas. The Bible concepts began to make furrows in his heart, drop seed and nurture growth.

One day he wrote to me, "I get into more and more Bible discussions. Actually, with your help, I'm becoming pretty good at it. But, really, the reason I'm writing is to tell you that Ed Haas is getting very interested in your Jesus Christ. Does He save Jews the same as He saves Gentiles?"

Ed made a trip to Lima. We had him at our house for dinner. After the meal, Juanita tactfully took the children upstairs.

Taking my Bible, I opened it and said, "Jew or Gentile, it's all the same to the Lord." He read these quotations, "There is no difference. For all have sinned, and come short of the glory of God" (Romans 3:22-23 KJV). "Christ died for our sins according to the scriptures.... He was buried.... He rose again the third day according to the scriptures" (1 Corinthians 15:3-4 KJV). "Whosoever shall call upon the name of the Lord shall be saved" (Romans 10:13, KJV).

That night this Jewish salesman knelt by our couch and invited Jesus Christ into his life!

He took to Christianity the same way he took to his job. He read the Bible intently, sent me many questions. He led his wife to the Lord and witnessed faithfully to others.

Ed Haas truly became my brother in Christ!

Two years later, I received a telephone call from Ed's wife in Stamford. She was sobbing, and I could scarcely make out her words.

"My husband has had a fatal heart attack," she told me. "He is dead."

My thoughts went back to that night in Rockford, Illinois, when the Holy Spirit so gently but firmly reminded me of the $4,000. I could have kept the money, of course.

But I thought of those customers who would not have been challenged. And I thought of Ed—hungering for something he could not explain, eager to reach out to the Savior!

Could it be that Ed Haas would not have otherwise made it to heaven!

"To obey," the Bible says, "is better than sacrifice" (1 Samuel 15:22, KJV).

It assuredly is!

WOODCHIPS

Nutshell

The God who designs each snowflake, who numbers the hairs of your head, is the God who rewards the smallest obedience with His blessing.

Branching out

As you progress in your own understanding of personal obedience, these suggestions might be of help to you:

1. Review once more Psalm 139:23-24. Invite the Holy Spirit to bring to light, or to clarify, items or areas in your life needing an act of your obedience.
2. Ask the Lord to give you deliverance from any fear, reluctance or apprehensions you may have.
3. Do you have a friend or loved one with whom you can share your thoughts, your concerns?

Stanley and Juanita, co-laborers in business and in Christian service.

Son-in-law Wes Little (left) shoulders major responsibility for business operation.

Shipping area in the plant.

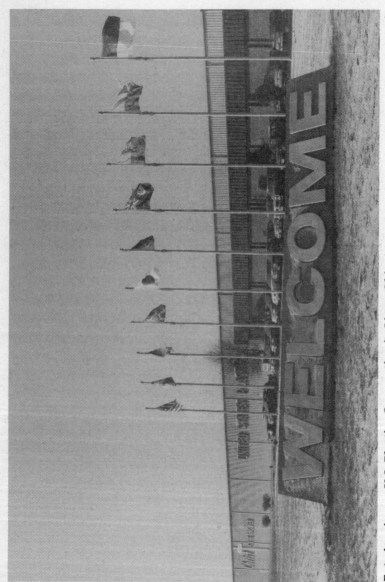

Exterior view — U.S. Plastics Corporation in Lima, Ohio.

Flags of many nations unfurl outside plant, attesting to the world-wide ministry of Tam products.

Cornerstone to the building attests: Property is a sacred trust from the Lord.

Passersby on Interstate 75 view this forceful witness. Several have come to Christ as the result of seeing those four words!

Motivation for all who work in the organization.

Nerve-Center is the large area where telephone orders are received and processed.

Popular hub of the business is the company store.

Juanita has handled payroll for many years.

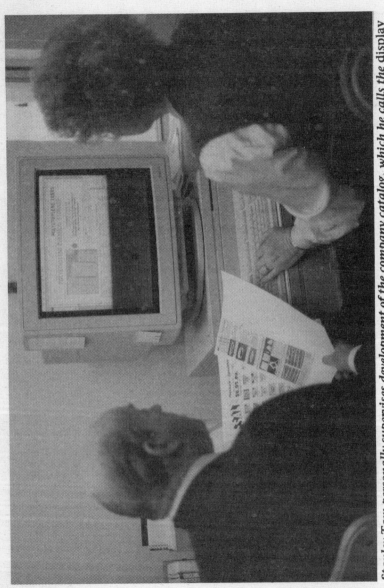

Stanley Tam personally supervises development of the company catalog, which he calls the display window for the company.

The boss at his desk. Many have been brought to Christ over the telephone!

An authentic Olympic gold medal was received from the mayor of Seoul, South Korea.

A few of the citations received from the multitudes who have benefitted from Stanley Tam's ministry through the years.

7

No Place
Like Home

Fathers, do not exasperate your children. Ephesians 6:4

When New Testament Christians selected a leader, one of the key requirements was that "he must manage his own family well and see that his children obey him with proper respect" (1 Timothy 3:4). That Scripture hints at much of the heartache and lack of power among contemporary Christians, leaders and lay alike!

God's Woodshed is not a treatise on family living, but I must affirm that it is one thing for parents to demand respect and another thing for them to earn it.

Love between parents and offspring is a natural emotion. Parents could be atheists and yet also be exemplary in their relationship to their children.

As a boy on the farm, I saw the affection between chicks and a mother hen. I would search the barn loft to discover where our mother cat had hidden her kittens, and watched for hours the love she displayed toward those tiny creatures. The same was true of cattle, horses and other animals.

In the case of humans, a deeply-committed Christian

life can contribute substantially to family relationships.

The son of one Christian family, himself now a recognized evangelical leader, says, "I never saw my parents quarrel. In times of strong disagreement, they would sit and calmly talk, each sharing Scriptures they had found meaningful and to the point. They were firm in their discipline of us children, yet always fair. They made sure we understood why they had made any given decision. When, rarely, they made unfair assessments, they always apologized."

Says another leader, "My wife and I have patterned our family life on the principles and practices I remember from my own childhood."

Motives are so important in family relationships. In counseling with Christian parents, one disturbing factor often emerges. Pressed to the fine edge of their motives, fathers and mothers will admit their first concern is selfishness. It is embarrassing at church and among their Christian friends to be the parents of children who are unsaved. Conversely, it becomes a matter of vanity for some to say, "My children are all believers."

So let me sound a warning!

I can be active in church, enjoy a commendable pew-size reputation, and yet have my soul cancer-ridden with pride, disobedience or unconfessed sin. And, when I do, my mate and children will see the difference—at times painfully—even though others, observing at a distance, do not.

I knew of one man who, at the age of 80, witnessed to his faith in Christ as Savior. He had lived a lifetime in unbelief, became an alcoholic, divorced his wife and grieved his mother's heart. His father was a lay Christian leader of national recognition who, outside his home, became known as a true man of faith. To his family, however, he was selfish, demanding and at times overtly cruel.

At the age of 15, the son told his mother, "If that's what

Christianity is, I don't ever want anything to do with it!"

And he didn't.

Not until the twilight years of this man's life were his mother's prayers answered, long after her own death.

One of my friends, an evangelist, told me of a heart-wrenching experience. He had spoken to a youth group in a town that also served as the headquarters of a small denomination. Following his message, a certain young man was among those who responded to the invitation.

"He asks to speak with you privately," the pastor told the speaker. "He seems very distressed about something. I told him to wait in my study."

My friend turned to go. The pastor touched his arm.

"I'm not sure what his problem is," he added, "but perhaps you should know that his father is the president of our denomination."

The university student stood waiting as my friend entered the pastor's study and gestured for the young man to sit.

"I don't know why I asked to talk to you," the student said. "I've kept something in my gut for a long time. I don't know if you can help me any."

"I'll try," said the evangelist.

Ten minutes passed. The two sat in silence. The young man opened and clenched his right fist, over and over, until he seemed to be preparing himself for a physical outburst of frustration and distress.

Finally, the evening's speaker said, "Look, we've been here long enough for me to have spoken and prayed with you. If you wish, you may go and I'll not mention details to anyone."

The student hesitated. "I thought maybe you could help me," he said, "but I don't know if anybody can."

"Well," countered my friend, "my head holds a lot of secrets. But don't feel obligated to share with me, just because you asked to see me."

Silence again.

Tactfully, the evangelist asked, "May I ask a personal question? Are you a Christian?"

This broke the ice.

"Sure I'm a Christian! Have been since I was no taller than a Sunday school chair. More than anything else in life, I want to be a real Christian!"

Again he hesitated. The two sat in silence another five minutes. The clenching and unclenching of the right fist continued in eloquent non-verbal expression.

"But...?"

"But I'm sick," the young man sprang to his feet, "sick, sick, sick of my dad's kind of Christianity!"

My friend also stood.

"I'm sure you know my dad. He's a big man with church people all over the country."

"Yes, I know of him," the startled evangelist managed to say, frightful of what he might hear next.

"Well, I'll tell you something. My dad's a saint among people who don't know him, but to Mom and us kids, he's a devil!"

With that the student stomped out of the room. My friend never saw him again.

What causes such a disturbed family life? I believe the answer lies not in emotional or physical incompatibility, but in a spiritual problem.

In dealing with spiritually troubled households, a counselor in our area uses a simple technique borrowed from the designs of geometry. He draws a triangle and places the name of the husband at one of the bottom angle points, the name of the wife at the other. At the top point of the triangle, he puts the name "Jesus Christ."

Gesturing first to the husband's name, then the wife's, then the name of Jesus, he says, "Any two people who can get through to Jesus Christ can get through to each other as well!"

He emphasizes something else, too.

Except in these modern times, when both parents work to maintain their lifestyles, mother has often been the pivotal parent in the home.

In actuality, however, the Bible indicates that father is to be the leader. Not dominant. Not an overlord. Just as any successful organization needs an administrator, so also does the home, and God intends fathers to fill that role (see Proverbs 3:11-12). Fathers are also to be the spiritual heads of their homes (see 1 Thessalonians 2:11-12) And, a facet so often missing, God intends fathers to be the channels through whom His love flows to their families (see Ephesians 5:33).

I think of these truths when, on weekend engagements, I look out at an audience of typical church folk.

"Lord," I silently pray, "help me to show these people a simple truth. Every human being was created with the capability and the capacity to receive and give out the abundance of Your love! Fulfillment in their lives can happen only when they experience this capability. It is hidden, unconfessed sin and indifference which hinder them from being and experiencing their spiritual birthright as Your children!"

I wonder, too, how many parents deny their children the blessing of vital faith because they, themselves, live a lie—professing to be right with God, hiding deceit in their hearts and living as models of disobedience before their children.

Am I saying that, if you come clean with the Lord, if you make your home truly Christ-centered, your family life will be perfect? Will your experience be akin to insulating your house from winter's blasts and summer's heat?

Not necessarily, either in your home or your personal life!

In fact, some of my occasions of greatest testing have come when, to the best of my knowledge, I had an unencumbered relationship between myself and the Lord. God was merely preparing me for future service and blessing.

We have four daughters. When our youngest, Candy, was a sophomore in college, she wrote to Juanita and me, "January 21 is your wedding anniversary. I've decided to come home and take you out to dinner. I'm free after lunch on Friday. I can drive back Sunday afternoon and be ready for my first class Monday."

"She shouldn't do that!" I said to Juanita. "Call and tell her we appreciate her thoughtfulness, but—"

My wife nudged me, held up the letter and said, "Read all of it, Stanley."

The letter continued, "We'll make it a double celebration, because I have something wonderful to tell you!"

"Uh, oh," I commented.

"Sounds serious," Juanita said. Her eyes sparkled as only a mother's eyes can on such occasions. Then she grew serious and added, "We've got to help her think sensibly. She has two more years of college."

Candy pulled into our driveway at five o'clock.

"Ready to go?" she sang out, entering the house. "I thought we'd eat at that restaurant I like so much over in Ada. Would you please drive, Daddy? Then I can tell you about my big surprise. If I wait to tell you after we get to the restaurant, I'll be too excited to eat."

As we headed east out of Lima, we expected Candy to begin talking. Instead, she sat mute in the back seat. I glanced at my wife. She looked at me with raised eyebrows. But neither of us spoke.

Finally, when we were almost to Maysville, our daughter began. "You're waiting to hear what I have to say," she half-whispered.

"We won't hear anything," her mother said gently, "unless you talk a little bit louder."

Silence again.

"We want to hear," Juanita prompted.

We passed through Maysville and came to the junction, where we turned to head north. A billboard advertised the restaurant as three miles farther, just at the outskirts of Ada.

"Mom, Dad," Candy began, measuring each word, "I've fallen in love."

"What?" my wife and I exclaimed in unison. Then Juanita quickly added, "That's wonderful!"

"It's about time, isn't it?" I said.

"Tells us about him," Juanita added.

My wife and I were now the excited ones, chattering like a couple of children. There was no traffic, so I slowed the car to a crawl.

"What's his name?" Juanita asked.

She gave us his name, and then blurted out, "He's asked me to marry him, and I told him yes."

"Is he a college student like you?" I inquired.

"N-no."

"He's a Christian?" Juanita asked.

"Oh, sure, Mom! You know me better than to ask that!"

We reached the restaurant and I pulled into a parking spot. But we all remained in the car.

"If he's not in college," my wife probed, "how old is he?"

"Thirty something...."

"Candy!" I spoke so loudly Juanita touched my knee. "Isn't that quite a spread in age?"

"You're not out of your teens," Juanita said quietly.

"But when you meet him, you'll understand," our daughter countered. "I go out with guys my age on campus, and they're such nerds. But he's different. He knows how to treat a girl on a date. He makes me feel like a queen."

We sounded her out further, learning that this chap was a divorced man with a house full of children.

"It's one thing to adjust to marriage," Juanita counseled. "But to come home from the honeymoon to a house full of children...."

"I'll be honored to raise his children for him," Candy insisted. "Wait until you meet him. Wait until you see how wonderful he is."

"It doesn't seem to me your mother and I have any business meeting this man," I said. Afterward, I was sorry for having spoken so bluntly.

Silence now permeated that car like a steel band at the plant drawn tight to secure one of our plastics' shipments.

In full honesty, I can affirm that I was concerned about our darling daughter. But I was concerned about Stanley Tam as well. What would people think? Our neighbors? At the plant? At church? When I stood up to speak at meetings?

"I should have known," I heard Candy mutter in disgust.

"Shall we go into the restaurant?" Juanita asked.

"I'm not hungry!" our daughter huffed.

We drove home. In utter silence. I had hardly stopped the car when Candy burst out and ran to the door. She had her own key and hurried inside to her room where she locked the door.

She didn't come down all the next day. Juanita tried to interest her in food but she only muttered incoherently.

Saturday night came and passed. Sunday morning, too. We always looked forward to having Candy attend worship with us when she returned for visits. But not this day.

Afternoon came and soon it would be time for a very disappointed and disgruntled young lady to drive back to college.

"Stanley!" Juanita prodded. "You can't just sit doing nothing!"

So I trudged up the stairs and knocked on the locked door.

"Umf!" Candy responded.

"Your mother and I want to have open minds," I said painfully. "Come down and let's talk about the situation."

Our daughter, bright-eyed, joined us in the living room. She had obviously read too much into my statement of wanting to be open minded.

I stammered for a few moments, never getting to the point. Candy began glancing at the clock. So I suggested that, as we always did when she left us, we go to our knees for a parting prayer. All three of us participated, although I can't remember one word that was uttered.

After our prayer, Juanita helped Candy get her things together. I pressed some money into our daughter's hand and gave her a dutiful kiss on the cheek. I thought I saw tears in her eyes as she headed straight to the door and outside, not looking back.

My wife and I stood at the window, watching. When her car was out of sight, I grasped Juanita by the shoulders and moved her back to where we had just knelt. Together, we poured out our hearts to the Lord, imploring Him to look after our baby daughter, asking His forgiveness for failures on our own part.

One month went by. Two months. Three.

My Thursday-noon prayer partner had recently gone through a similar circumstance. Art's son, a fine young Christian, fell in love with a lovely young lady who wasn't a believer. Within a week of the wedding—we believe in direct answer to our prayers—they broke up.

Now it was my turn.

Every Thursday, Art and I met for prayer. Every morning and every night, Juanita and I prayed together. Again and again at work, I would stop what I was doing, bow at my desk and ask the Lord to help our dear Candy.

"I ask for You not to let her miss Your will, Lord," I

prayed.

That prayer really convicted me because I had to admit that, so long as our daughter obeyed the Lord, whatever happened would have His blessing.

I felt a new tenderness come to my heart. I regretted the harsh words I had spoken to Candy. As a result, I became much more tolerant toward our staff. Weekends, when on speaking engagements, I sensed a difference, a warmth and an abundant unction.

Yet I held back.

One night Juanita said in tears, "I took this matter to the Lord today. I asked Him to carry out His will and to give me the courage to accept whatever that may be!"

Thank God for Christian women like my Juanita!

Candy wrote as before, telling us about classes, her friends in the dorm and activities at the church she attended. She didn't mention her boyfriend. We tried to be loving and positive in our letters to her, giving hints of our willingness to stand by her decision.

Then, at last, she wrote us with the real news: "Mom and Dad, I love you so much! You can never know how much. I wouldn't do anything to hurt you. But I also know you don't want me to hinder myself just to please you. I've been praying much about the future, about how things could be 20 years from now. Thank you for all the lessons you've taught me about seeking God's will for our lives. Well, that's what I've been doing. And I know I've done what the Lord wants me to do, not just what would please you. I have broken up with Gary."

What a mighty answered prayer! What a maturity in our daughter!

And what a change in me—my ministry has never been the same since!

WOODCHIPS

Nutshell

The principles by which an individual lives as a vital Christian relate to homes and families. Wrong actions and attitudes in the home need correcting and cleansing the same as with our inward lives.

Branching out

If you are a family member, give thought to the following:

1. Read Ephesians 5:22-31; 6:1-4.
2. Do these principles prevail in your home?
3. Is there anything you can do to make Christian principles more effective in your home? Offer your bodies as living sacrifices, holy and pleasing to God. Romans 12:1

8

Master Controlled

Offer your bodies as living sacrifices, holy and pleasing to God.
Romans 12:1

My grandfather was an itinerant entertainer. Back in the days of hand-wind phonographs and country schoolhouses, long before television and even radio, he hitched up a horse to a spring wagon. He and Grandma took to the country dirt roads and trekked from community to community putting on performances.

Grandpa specialized in magic and could hold farmers spellbound for hours with sleight-of-hand tricks. He would pull eggs out of a young boy's ear. He might learn who the school bully was, reach into that child's desk and bring out a cute little doll. Then he'd tease the blushing lad for playing with girls' toys.

But of all of Grandpa's skills, nothing so gripped my attention as his puppet show. He had two characters called Punch and Judy. Hiding behind a stage, so people didn't see him or his hands, he manipulated the puppets with strings. His puppets appeared to be very clever. They could sing. They got into arguments. They even began to fight at times, until either Grandpa or Grandma separated them.

Punch and Judy would sprawl lifeless in the box Grandma had prepared for them, coming to life only when they came under Grandpa's skillful control.

That's the way the Christian life is meant to be.

No, believers aren't puppets. The God Who so masterfully designed creation as to forbid even duplicate snowflakes, blesses each of us with a uniqueness all our own. But if we want to succeed as human beings—and as Christians in particular—we must put ourselves into His control.

In short, we need to be master controlled.

This relationship doesn't make us super-Christians. Nor are we better than others. We won't wear visible halos!

What happens is that the Holy Spirit takes charge of our lives, leading us into opportunities, steering us from wrong and making us sensitive to those situations which other Christians seem to miss.

To be master controlled, I must be clean. And to be characterized by this purity, I may need to spend some time in God's woodshed. Not a back room of punishment, but an experience which causes me to search my heart and make right the wrongs hidden there.

As a young Christian, sincerely striving to find God's very best for my life, I became keenly aware that the Lord wanted me to witness. I, who was so shy that I preferred overcast days so as not to be frightened by my own shadow, was to walk up to people and tell them they needed salvation!

People today tend to pooh-pooh street meetings. We cheapen the gospel, some insist, if we stand out in public places and sing or give Christian witness.

Wait a minute. Does it cheapen a business product when someone goes public and gives samples to passers-by? No! Then can't we likewise find an appealing way to showcase the gospel?

One blustery afternoon, a so-called fanatic stood on a London street with an open Bible and loudly declared the gospel. A young man happened by. He was a school dropout involved in drugs. He made a quick decision that the preacher must be nuts!

"Let's give him a rough time," the young man suggested to a friend.

"Naw," the friend replied, "I've got better things to do."

As he walked away, this friend called back, laughing, "Be careful or you'll get saved!"

The friend decided to listen for a few moments. He became keenly interested in the speaker's logic. Instead of causing a disturbance, he lingered to ask further questions. Soon, there on the street, he opened his heart to the Lord Jesus.

That young man joined Operation Mobilization and subsequently established his own outreach organization. Although he never finished high school, he is in a special program at a Big Ten university, working on his Ph.D.!

"I don't know what would have happened to me if it hadn't been for that street preacher!" summarizes this new creature in Christ.

Is my conclusion that, when a Christian becomes master controlled, he or she will head for the road with pockets full of tracts and a Bible the size of a Sears Roebuck catalog?

The evangelist from London had designed some innovative procedures for street witnessing. I don't think I could ever be like him. But when I'm master controlled, things do happen that I would never have predicted!

I've said that I'm by nature shy. Once I knew for sure that I was a child of God, I became convinced that I must witness. If I had gone out onto the street to preach, the first pair of staring eyes would have melted me like wax.

I ran across one fellow who was sheer boldness from the

top of his head to the spit shine of his shoes. He shared the gospel with anyone who came near him. When he rode a train, he would go from one end to the other passing out tracts.

A conductor once put him off for refusing to stop, and this man spent the evening witnessing to people in that town. Next day, he caught the same train and continued his journey—and his evangelizing.

Stanley Tam could no more do that than fly!

But I could do something else.

In those days, Christian films were in their infancy. I heard of a man in Chicago who had established a small production and distribution ministry. I went to see him.

"What I have in mind," I told him, "is to get a projector and some films and then see if people will let me come to their homes and show them."

I remember the tears that came to that Christian's eyes. He was thrilled to think of his movies being used in this manner.

His ministry featured a number of short subjects, each with a gospel witness. I selected two of his productions. Then he helped me procure a projector.

Back in Lima, I secured the names of parents whose children attended our church's Sunday school, and then placed some phone calls. Those were years long before television.

"Come to my home and show us a motion picture? Free?" I would be asked as I made these contact. "What's the wrinkle? What're you selling—vacuum cleaners? Insurance?"

"We just put a roof on the house," said another person, "so I don't have enough extra money to buy my children an ice cream cone. But if it's free...."

And another, "My wife keeps the checkbook and she's tighter than the D-string on my banjo. You're sure there's no money involved?"

"I'm not selling anything," I would tell people, "and I couldn't accept any payment if you offered it. I attend the Alliance church here in Lima, and they gave me your name and address."

"Coming to preach to us?"

"No, to show you a Christian film."

Some people may have initially turned me down, because our calendars were at variance, but the majority of those I called extended an invitation.

"I'll have the missis bake us a batch of oatmeal cookies," said one congenial gentleman. "Bakes them just like her mother used to."

As I pulled up in front of the first residence and took out my projector and films, and headed toward the front door, I prayed, "Lord, You know how shy I am. Yet I'm sure You laid it on my heart to witness, so please help me do it."

I was so frightened, so self-conscious that I stood a long moment summoning courage to ring the doorbell. Perspiration stood out on my forehead. My mouth went straw dry.

But as I stood there in anguish, I made a wonderful discovery. When I obey God, when I take the initiative—however faltering—to do what He asks, I receive added strength and wisdom. The promise God gave to Joshua came to my mind: "Have I not commanded you? Be strong and courageous. Do not be terrified; do not be discouraged, for the Lord your God will be with you wherever you go" (Joshua 1:9). I knew God would never ask me to do anything without also providing the capability of doing it!

I also discovered that, when I am obedient to the Holy Spirit's guidance, I can expect to be led in my witness to those whom the Holy Spirit has prepared to receive God's Word.

More than any other truth or experience, that fact underlies and undergirds my adventures in soul winning. The Apostle Paul told his followers that he and his associates were "only servants, through whom you came to believe—as the Lord has assigned to each his task. I planted the seed, Apollos watered it, but God made it grow" (1 Corinthians 3:5-6).

When I witness, God doesn't look to me as the soul winner.

That's the Holy Spirit's job. People are the tools, the instruments, through whom the Holy Spirit does His work.

As I state in my autobiography, *God Owns My Business*, "I'm convinced that every Christian can be a soul winner. You may not be able to bring every person you contact to a knowledge of Christ, but you can plant the seed or nurture the seed. You can be a stepping stone. Only the Holy Spirit can bring a person to salvation. You and I are merely the tools used to carry the message."

I didn't win anyone to the Lord in the first few homes I visited. I showed the movies and spoke about our church. Even so, I made yet one more discovery. The people whom I visited were eager to have Christian friends. They spoke of believers as something special, people they could trust, people willing to help others in need. Several began to attend our church and subsequently were converted to a personal faith in Christ.

I cannot overemphasize the fact that, when people seek to be master controlled by the Holy Spirit, they gain confidence in the realization that they truly are "laborers together with God" (1 Corinthians 3:9).

I learned during those fledgling days of witnessing that I must never mistake inexperience for inability. In no other area of life is it more true that practice makes perfect!

With each visit, my confidence grew and my shyness decreased. When I returned home, I would lie awake in my bed marveling at the progress I was making. God has blessed me wonderfully in business. I'm no master merchandiser, but son-in-law Wes and I have put into practice a number of sales approaches which are quite successful. It's always a joy, when five o'clock comes around, to look at the day's statistics and see how well we've done. But I would willingly go bankrupt and be a bag boy at the local supermarket if doing so would cause more people to be led to the Lord!

I never played on a championship football team or emerged as high point man in a basketball game. Real athletes, when they reach my age, must have many pleasant memories of their exploits. What I remember, and often think about, is my first taste of harvest! Nothing in life can exceed the joy, the sense of attainment or the depth of fulfillment that results from bringing a lost soul into the outreaching arms of the Lord Jesus!

I remember visiting a middle-class home of people whom I had not met. They had been recommended by one of the members of our church. Both the husband and wife were especially friendly. I had found a home where hearts had been prepared by the Holy Spirit!

The wife, I subsequently learned, had accepted the Lord as Savior years earlier but followed her husband's leading in not participating in religious activities.

As I showed the film, I noticed how intently the husband watched. It made me nervous, because I figured I would need to ask him if he wanted to open his heart to Christ, and my courage hadn't been advanced to that point!

After turning off the projector, I puttered with it for a few moments. I silently prayed, "Lord, I'm scared. Please help me!"

I had forgotten how sure I can be of the Holy Spirit's guidance!

As I was still rewinding the film, the man turned to me. He cleared his throat but kept silent. So did I. My tongue was a fist-size knot in my throat!

"You know," the man began at last, "when I was a kid, I went to Sunday school regularly. I knew dozens of Bible verses, including just about every one in that movie you just showed us.

"Years back, my wife and I used to go to church. We were even fairly regular. Sometimes I had a lot of interest in Christianity. I figured that maybe somebody would talk to me about it. No one ever did. Then we sort of drifted away."

My heard pounded like a jackhammer and my breath came in spurts. I managed to stammer, "You could become a Christian tonight, right now, just as you saw happen in the film."

He looked straight at me. I saw deep spiritual hunger in his eyes.

"Why don't you do it, Frank?" his wife urged.

"I believe I will!" Frank responded.

If my car had wings, I would have flown a mile high over Lima on my way home that night.

"I did it, Juanita!" I exclaimed as I burst into the door. "I led a man to Christ tonight! It's the greatest experience of my whole life."

Having once tasted the joy of bringing someone to the Lord, I continued my witnessing with increased fervor. Defying all fear, I could approach strangers or acquaintances and invite them to consider my Savior.

I've heard people speak of the "offence of the gospel." I know what they mean. The gospel can be so assaulting to people steeped in sin, unbelief or indifference that they want nothing to do with it. The Bible says, "The message of the cross is foolishness to those who are perishing" (1 Corinthians 1:18). It's equally true, however, that sometimes the people who witness, rather than the gospel itself, are what cause the stumbling block.

In my early experiences, I passed out tracts to anyone who

happened to come near me. Other times, such as while waiting for a plane or train, I would approach someone who was sitting alone and begin my witness.

On one occasion, a rather polite-looking gentleman became livid with anger and snarled, "Don't sneak around trying to make fools out of people. If I want to hear about religion, I'll go to church."

He had hardly finished speaking when I realized that I had approached him on my own. I hadn't been led by the Holy Spirit.

I have much to learn about sharing my faith and being master controlled, but I do know from many experiences that I can depend on the Spirit. In fact, I've learned always to depend on His guidance. For all my years of seasoning, I'm still a bit too reserved to pick prospects at random and begin giving them the sin-suffer-and-repent routine.

Dr. Walter Wilson, a much loved Kansas City family physician, is known by many as one of America's foremost soul winners. Based on the times I met him and heard him speak, I suspect he was blessed with considerably more courage than am I.

"When I go 'fishing' for the Lord," he has said, "I often use bait. If I stand at the corner waiting for a bus, and another person comes alongside me, I smile pleasantly. Sometimes this person opens the conversation and gives me a chance to witness. Other times I will say, 'Hasn't the Lord given us nice weather to enjoy?' If the Holy Spirit has prepared that person's heart, a witnessing opportunity will occur as easily and naturally as a discussion about the temperature."

In my own case, I tend to be more reserved.

I have discovered, through experience, that even I can be led into opportune moments for sharing my faith. It's thrilling to think of common, ordinary Stanley Tam being master controlled and to know that my friends can be also!

A typical example occurred on a flight from South America at a time when travelers cleared customs in San Juan, Puerto Rico. As Juanita and I waited in line, an Army sergeant stood behind us. We struck up casual conversation.

Reboarding the plane, I noticed that Sergeant Mackenzie was among the passengers. In that instant, the Holy Spirit whispered to me, "Stanley, I want you to witness to that man."

"But Lord," I countered, "not on this airplane. The circumstances aren't suitable for soul winning."

What I meant was that we were on a tourist flight, jammed together like sardines in a can. I was in a window seat and I didn't see how I could make my way over to Sergeant Mackenzie.

"If you don't witness to him," the silent voice seemed to say, "no one else ever will, and Sergeant Mackenzie won't go to heaven."

The pilot started the engines, moved onto the runway and took off. Since the "Fasten Seat Belts" indicator was lit, I had a temporary excuse for sitting still. Soon, however, passengers were permitted to move about. Not me, though. The man on our aisle promptly put back his seat, stretched out his feet and went to sleep. I was locked in place!

I, too, tried to doze. But my eyes kept drifting toward the soldier who sat looking intently up the aisle as though engrossed in thought.

"That Army man we talked to," I whispered to Juanita.

"He was nice," she said, nodding.

"He may be a lost soul, and I feel I've got to talk with him."

"But we're so packed in here," my wife said. "You'll need to wait until we reach Miami."

"There may not be any chance then."

Juanita glanced around at the jam-packed cabin, and then looked at me in sympathy but with no further suggestions.

I sat for several moments. Every time I looked across the passengers, the Holy Spirit increasingly urged me to obey. Once I almost got up, but the man on the aisle slumped further forward, his body blocking my path like a big door.

Juanita browsed through the latest copy of *Reader's Digest* for a few moments. Then she yawned and her eyes closed.

I also shut my eyes. But all I could do was pray. "Okay Lord," I said, "I'll witness to this guy if You will arrange it."

No sooner had I prayed than the Army man rose, squeezed himself over to the aisle and went to the front of the cabin. He stood examining a map of the Caribbean. Our helpful captain had been identifying various islands as we flew over them.

I nudged Juanita, awakening her.

I pointed to the front.

She smiled and nodded.

It was awkward, getting to the aisle, but I managed. In moments I stood beside Sergeant Mackenzie.

"Do you know where we are?" I asked.

"Here," he said, pointing to an island.

We both looked for a moment.

Then, less tactfully than I would have wished, I said, "God has laid you on my heart, and I've been praying for you."

He turned abruptly to me. In that first moment, I expected a negative response. Instead, happiness showed in his eyes.

"Are you interested in spiritual things?" I asked.

"Yes, I am," he responded, the warmth and eagerness lingering in his facial expression.

It took some jockeying, but Juanita graciously went over and occupied Sergeant Mackenzie's place, so he and I could sit together.

I reached for my briefcase and, before opening it, asked, "Mind if I show you some things in my Bible?"

"That would be great," he replied.

During the next hour a shy, reluctant but master-controlled Stanley Tam led Sergeant Bob Mackenzie to a personal knowledge of the Lord Jesus Christ!

After returning home, I became concerned about Bob and wrote to him. His letter of response contained these words. "You ask if I know I received the Lord Jesus Christ as my personal Savior there on the plane. I'm glad to tell you I did. I'm following the Lord and going to church every Sunday."

Yes, anyone can truly be master controlled!

But the Lord knows how very human people are, so there will often be a price to pay. I may need to make a trip to the woodshed. For, when I sincerely aspire to be master controlled, I can expect the Holy Spirit to keep close watch on my thoughts, motives and experiences.

The absolute prerequisite for being master controlled is to be clean. Not perfect, but clean. Through recent years, the Lord has brought me often to a place of reckoning where, to qualify for the Holy Spirit's purifying and guidance, I've had to make things right.

As you ask the Lord to master control your life, if the experience is new to you, you may evidence some uncertainty. You'll wonder if it's really true that God's hand is on your life. Maybe your lack of experience will be behind such emotions. More likely, it will be Satan at work, as I described in Chapter Two. Always remember that the devil must not upstage the Holy Spirit in your life. That's why you need to rebuke him and bind him daily!

Much joy will come to your life, as your pursue the reality of being master controlled. You may even experience some side benefits. I did, while Ken Anderson and I were working on this book.

Two men from a bank in Lima, one of them the manager, came to see me. They wanted us to be their customers and were unaware of our policy not to borrow money. While they thought they were meeting us for business reasons, they really fell into the pulse of the Holy Spirit's control of my life!

As a layman I cannot perform weddings, but I do occasionally conduct funerals. "When we attended Merl May's last rites," the bank manager said, "my wife and I were quite intrigued to find you in charge."

Mr. May, a millionaire, was the former chairman of that bank's board of directors.

"I had the privilege of leading Mr. May to the Lord before he passed away," I said. "His nephew is Joe Leatherman, a man I pointed to Christ several years ago. It was Joe who asked me to speak to Mr. May.

"You see," I continued, "the way of salvation is for all— rich man, poor man—it makes no difference. God sees every human as a lost sinner needing salvation. You may remember how at the funeral I explained the pathway to heaven as I described the decisions Mr. May made before he died."

Then I carefully outlined those steps again.

"First, recognize yourself a sinner. 'All have sinned and fall short of the glory of God' (Romans 3:23). Then, recognize what God has done to save you from your sins. The Bible says, 'Christ died for our sins according to the Scriptures, that he was buried, that he was raised on the third day according to the Scriptures' (1 Corinthians 15:3, 4). Next, you accept Jesus into your heart and life, because the Bible promises us that 'everyone who calls on the name of the Lord will be saved' (Romans 10:13)."

I hesitated a moment.

Then I asked, "If you died today, where would you go?"

"To heaven!" the bank manager replied, catching me by surprise. He then explained. "I prayed what you called the sinner's prayer during Mr. May's funeral service. I invited

Christ into my life!"

I was overjoyed.

Then I turned to the second man and asked. "What about you? Have you trusted Christ as your Savior?"

He shook his head to indicate no.

"Would you like to?"

He nodded convincingly.

In the next moments, under the Holy Spirit's master control, a rather retiring, and at times shy, Christian by the name of Stanley Tam led this precious soul to a saving knowledge of the Lord Jesus Christ.

WOODCHIPS

Nutshell

Living a master-controlled Christian life seems abnormal to some people only because so few believers evidence such a life. But any Christian, who will meet God's conditions, can be master controlled.

Branching out

Follow these steps toward achieving the master-controlled Christian life:

1. Read Romans 12:1-2. Let this be the foundation for your search.

2. Pray this prayer: "Lord, I can do nothing to merit your salvation. I can only trust in Your mercy, forgiveness and grace through my faith in Jesus Christ. I now realize I cannot live the master-controlled life in my own strength. I invite the Holy Spirit to take full control of my body and mind. I will follow His guidance, through the instructions I find in the Bible."

3. Read 2 Peter 3:18. Make this verse your goal for the master-controlled life.

9

The Skill of
Tongue
Management

A word aptly spoken is like apples of gold in settings of silver.
Proverbs 25:11

I heard of two business partners who couldn't get along with or without each other. Invariably, when they discussed their business affairs, one of them would say something that incited the other and caused both to launch into a tirade. Finally, the two hit upon a solution. Whenever they met to confer, each placed a $20 bill on the conference table. If one of them raised his voice, the other collected both twenties.

The plan worked.

Certainly all will agree that discipline of the tongue plays a major role in being master controlled. I have often been brought up short, in times of my own bad attitudes, by the Bible's counsel that "the fruit of the Spirit is love, joy, peace, patience, kindness, goodness, faithfulness, gentleness and self- control" (Galatians 5:22, 23).

During the Gulf War, Americans boasted about the superior accuracy and fire power of weapons available to coalition forces. A bomb could supposedly have been dropped into the hind pocket of the Iraqi dictator. My heart ached to think of the lives lost, the bodies maimed. I am not a pacifist but neither do I glory in the devastating consequences of war.

But let me suggest something.

General Norman Schwarzkopf and his coalition forces had neither weapons nor ammunition capable of inflicting the hurt and havoc lurking in the human tongue! An Old Testament prophet talks about those whose "tongue is a deadly arrow; it speaks with deceit. With his mouth each speaks cordially to his neighbor, but in his heart he sets a trap for him" (Jeremiah 9:8). And a New Testament writer cautions us to "consider what a great forest is set on fire by a small spark. The tongue also is a fire" (James 3:5-6).

Obviously, then, a Christian cannot expect to effectively witness, or to be a help and encouragement to others, if that Christian's tongue is like a rifle loaded and cocked and waiting for a target.

When I think of being master controlled, I must put high on my list the control of my speech. Few Christians go around with their fists clenched, waiting for an excuse to punch somebody in the mouth. Many of God's children, however, strike with the quickness of a cobra when cause arises to spew ugliness about or against others. I cannot expect the blessing of God and the guidance of the Holy Spirit unless my "conversation be always full of grace, seasoned with salt" (Colossians 4:6). Indeed, God's Word cautions us further that "if anyone considers himself religious and does not keep a tight reign on his tongue, he deceives himself and his religion is worthless" (James 1:26).

A friend of mine had tongue troubles. He rarely took the initiative in word-sniping, but he was loaded and ready to respond when someone fired at him. He also suffered from that prevalent human malady known as gossip.

"What I have done," he relates, "is to silently program two words into my thought patterns: Shut and Up! This concept works wonders! When something triggers my temper, or if malicious conversation occurs in my presence, I silently speak those two words to myself."

Two problems lie volatile in every human tongue—the outbreak of temper and the spreading of gossip. In my opinion, the latter is the devil's counterpart to witnessing!

When I share my faith with others, I become the Lord's mouthpiece in using my tongue to enrich the lives of those the Holy Spirit sends across my path. When I gossip, however, I do the opposite! I've never seen any statistics on the subject, but I've wondered whether gossip is more frequently based on truth or on error. My guess would be that 30 percent of the subject matter involved in gossip is accurate while a good 70 percent would never earn a jury's guilty verdict!

I try to avoid all hearsay-infested conversation, but the one topic of gossip I loathe above others is the subject of immorality. The devil sees to it that nowhere do truth and fiction become more lethally entangled than in scandals involving sex. Many Christians seem to put aside the Bible's clear teaching that, in the theology of Jesus (see Matthew 5:27-28), lustful thoughts and immoral acts are one and the same!

In fact, I sometimes wonder if God sees any difference between the committing of adultery and the spreading of malicious gossip!

On one of my speaking engagements, I stayed in the home of a couple active in the church where I was speaking. Coming down to breakfast one morning, I found the husband and wife in the living room. She was sobbing, and her husband was at a loss for words by which to comfort her.

Seeing me, the man said, "We just got a telephone call. We had a former pastor who was quite close to us." He gestured to his wife. "Laura and his wife were like sisters."

The wife now burst into convulsive sobbing. Her husband laid a comforting hand on her shoulder. She brushed it away. So he stood and motioned for me to follow him into the next room.

"Brother Lowrie would perhaps still be our pastor," he said, "except for what happened. His wife, Jen, was a vivacious sort. She put a wonderful spark into our congregation when they first came."

He hesitated, and then continued. "A woman in our church, who preferred center stage for herself, became very jealous. She kept a hawk's eye on everything the pastor's wife did and criticized Jen if she so much as sneezed while somebody else was praying.

"This woman claimed she came into our fellowship room at church one night before a couples' club meeting, and found Jen and one of our men embracing. True or false, I don't know.

"Anyway, she first came to Laura and me, and we begged her to keep her mouth shut. We suggested meeting privately with the couple. If sin was involved, they could talk it out with the Lord. We suggested that maybe we wouldn't even speak to the pastor, not at first anyway, especially if we learned that nothing clandestine was going on. The man involved had recently lost his wife through divorce, and everybody felt sorry for him.

"Instead of following our suggestion, this woman spread the story across the whole church. It got to be a big scene, with the poor guy and the pastor's wife getting up in front of all of us and asking forgiveness, although they insisted their involvement was in no way what the gossip described!

"Pastor Lowrie offered to resign, but everybody liked him so much that they begged him to stay. So he did, for awhile.

"Jen, the pastor's wife, went into a shell. Sometimes three

or four weeks in a row, she wouldn't even show up. The guy involved quit the church and, frankly, I don't know what happened to him. Left town, I think. Well, the story grew until Pastor Lowrie did resign and took a church in another state.

"We kept in touch by telephone—Laura with Jen, and I with Pastor Lowrie. We even went to their new city once to see them. I almost wish we hadn't, because Jen went to pieces at the sight of us. We must have brought back too many painful memories.

"Even so, we kept in touch. We understood how the ordeal had completely changed Jen, made her a very deeply hurt person. Then this morning the telephone rang...."

His voice faltered.

He bit his lip.

"It was Pastor Lowrie. When he awakened this morning, Jen was gone. He found her in the bathroom. Slumped over the tub. Dead."

"Heart attack?" I asked.

"Suicide."

What a painful, terrible recourse. Had this cruel gossip not been started or spread, perhaps the story would have a different ending.

My tongue can be as much a menace as anyone else's. That's why every day I ask God to help me submit my mind and tongue to the Holy Spirit's control!

Let me tell you how the Lord took me to His woodshed because of my temper.

During World War II, we received a notice from our post office. Due to its short staff, and because of our location, we would no longer receive deliveries. We had heavy volume of both correspondence and shipments, so this meant sending a truck to the post office every morning. Because our mail is so precious to us, I elected myself to the job.

The man in charge of the post office's rear door was

slow as molasses. I would ring the bell and wait as much as a quarter hour to pick up our mail. One morning, delayed getting away from our place, my fuse was already burning short when I rang the back door bell. After waiting a full 15 minutes, I stepped up to the window and peeked inside.

There stood my irritant, reading the morning paper!

I banged so hard on the glass it's a wonder I didn't break it. He looked at me and sighed. It was obvious that our feelings toward each other were of the same stripe!

Finally he came onto the dock. I lit into him with a tirade. I didn't use profanity, because such words have no place in my vocabulary. But my heart can be just as profane, even though my tongue avoids four-letter words!

"Do you realize how much it costs me to come here to the post office?" I ranted. "I'm the president of our company and my time is worth a lot of money! Every month, you rob me of at least $100! If I sent the post office a bill, you'd lose your job! I'll tell you one thing, my friend, if you do lose your job, don't come crying to my place. I wouldn't hire you. It'd cost me money to have a drone like you on our staff!"

My words melted him down like a candle. His wimpy manner caused me to dislike him all the more.

As I drove away with our letters and packages that morning, the Lord said to me, "You're a Christian, aren't you, Stanley?"

"Of course I am!"

The Lord was smiting my conscience for the wrong I had done through my unsanctified attitude!

I knew the Lord wanted me to apologize immediately. Deep in my heart I wanted to as well.

But I didn't.

I promised the Lord, however, that the next time I came to the post office, I would apologize to the man, ask his forgiveness, give him a word of testimony.

The following morning when I came for our mail, a new face appeared at the door.

"What happened to that fellow who was here before?" I asked.

"He found another job," the postal worker told me.

Ordinarily, I might have said something about "good riddance," but my conscience struck me mute. It bothered me for awhile. Then I dismissed the incident from my mind.

Or thought I did!

Several months later, a Baptist pastor called, said he had to be out-of-town the next Sunday and asked if I would I fill in for him.

As I walked into that church, the Sunday school was just dismissing. Guess who the superintendent was? The man I had demeaned at the post office!

Our eyes met.

In that moment, it was as though we were back in time at the post office and I had just finished cutting him to shreds. He turned away. I knew I should pursue him, but I didn't.

As I sat on the platform at the worship service, this man seated himself in a pew. Our eyes met once more.

"You'll be wasting your time this morning," a voice seemed to whisper, "unless you go down to him and apologize."

Again I held back.

The opening procedures passed quickly. The church chairman, who was directing the service, got up to introduce me.

"I think we would all agree," he said, "that one of the most exemplary Christians in Lima is our guest speaker this morning."

I looked out at the former postal employee. He looked intently at me. Obviously, he didn't think of Stanley Tam as exemplary.

I was back in Gods's woodshed once again!

"When you get up to the pulpit," said that voice again, "you'll have an ideal opportunity to apologize."

"Apologize?" I almost gasped aloud. "In public?"

"Yes, Stanley."

"But, Lord, I'm a guest here. I've never been at this church before. I can't put on a scene in front of all these people."

The introduction concluded. The chairman turned and gestured for me to step to the pulpit. But I just sat there, pulverized. The ex-postman sat there, too, and I was sure I saw malice in his eyes! My heart leaped to my throat, pounding like an air hammer. My tongue was so dry I wondered if I could utter a word.

"Mr. Tam," the church chairman prompted, clearing his throat. He gestured a second time.

I stumbled to my feet and to the pulpit. As I did, the man I had demeaned also got up and walked briskly to the back, leaving the sanctuary. I took this initially as a reprieve and sighed with relief.

But as I began my message, every word seemed to bounce back at me. I lost my train of thought a couple of times. The audience became restless. The subject of my message was spiritual power but I, myself, felt like a burned out battery.

Then, just as I said, "If you want power as a Christian, you must live a clean life," the door at the back opened and the man re-entered!

I watched him a moment, then closed my Bible. "Your Sunday school superintendent knows some cleansing is needed in my life this morning," I managed to say.

I left the platform and went down the aisle to the ex-postman.

You could have heard a feather fall.

The audience listened and watched, as I poured out my heart in sincere apology. It was sheer agony, at first, but then something wonderful happened. Strength and peace came to me from resources beyond myself! "It is God who arms me with strength," the Bible assures believers in Psalm 18:32. Also, "the fruit of righteousness is sown in peace" (James 3:18 KJV).

"Will you please forgive me?" I asked.

"Sure, Mr. Tam!" he responded. "I will!" Even as we spoke, a spirit of revival spread across that audience. Many others did as I had done, making right the wrongs they had left unattended between themselves and family or friends.

What blessings await us if we obey the Lord and take the initiative to honor Him!

I thank God for the lessons He is teaching me about how I use my tongue. I've had to apologize for sharp words spoken to my wife, to my children and to people in our company.

And, whenever I've done it, God has seemed to turn on the spigot of His blessing in my heart!

Any Christian who desires God's best must deal with the tongue situation. Actions are important. Reactions even more so. But an unruly tongue can be like a culprit's paintbrush slashed across an artist's canvas! "A word aptly spoken," the Bible says, "is like apples of gold in settings of silver" (Proverbs 25:11). The Bible also speaks of some cases where the tongue is "a deadly arrow" (Jeremiah 9:8). How appropriately then for God to say, "Whoever would love life and see good days must keep his tongue from evil and his lips from deceitful speech" (1 Peter 3:10).

Through the years, I have developed a helpful antidote against the wrongful use of my tongue. Each day, I endeavor to give at least two compliments to people with whom I associate. I have found that the more I use my tongue for good, the less inclined I am to speak words I will later regret. I also have promised God that, if I lose my temper, I will apologize. This vow has rewarded me with wonderful victory over my temper!

WOODCHIPS

Nutshell

Are you perhaps like a lot of Christians, with "speech problems"? Take heart! One of the most delectable fruits of obedience is the graciousness of speech that can develop through our lives.

Branching out

For a more Christian vocabulary and manner of speaking, consider the following:

1. Monitor your own speech for a day. Listen to yourself. See if you approve of what you hear.

2. Make your speech a key item of daily prayer. Consider using Psalm 19:14 as your guideline and goal!

3. Take note of what you hear others say and, before you judge, ask yourself if similar attributes—both good or bad—characterize your speech.

10

VIP Status

Because of your wealth your heart has become proud. Ezekiel 28:4

As a businessman, I have achieved some measure of success. Several years ago, the Lord showed me the reason why. While reading my Bible one morning, I came across this verse: "Remember the Lord your God, for it is he who gives you the ability to produce wealth" (Deuteronomy 8:18).

I am convinced that no one achieves true success outside the will of God. When prosperity is obtained solely through human initiative and capability, the experience of wise King Solomon becomes applicable. A man of many accomplishments, Solomon wrote, "When I surveyed all that my hands had done and what I had toiled to achieve, everything was meaningless, a chasing after the wind" (Ecclesiastes 2:11). The Psalmist wisely wrote, "Unless the Lord builds the house, its builders labor in vain" (Psalm 127:1).

When I hear people speak of their jobs as a rat race or a Monday-through-Friday drag, a sadness touches my heart. "May the favor of the Lord our God rest upon us," the Psalmist prayed. "Establish the work of our hands" (Psalm 90:17).

Work should be a joy for every Christian. Our attitudes, our sharing, our outreach to others—all of these can find abundant outlets through daily labor!

I'm not, in any sense, a workaholic. Yet my idea of fun is succeeding in business, watching inventory expand and seeing the profit margin increase month by month and year by year. While I make no claims of humility, one of my urgent concerns is to be sure my lifestyle coincides with the Bible's admonition that "whether you eat or drink or whatever you do, do it all for the glory of God" (1 Corinthians 10:31).

Pride seems to be the reason Lucifer, the high angel in heaven, became Satan, the CEO of hell—the one whose continuing motive is to prevent you and me from becoming the kind of Christians you and I have the right to be! (see Isaiah 14:12-15).

There are no VIPs on God's roster of servants. The millionaire and the person at the lathe are the same in His sight. A fascinating book, *In Search of Excellence*, by authors Peters and Waterman, details the way in which 60 American corporations broke down the wall between front offices and work force. In one corporation, designated parking slots were eliminated. The president, arriving for work each morning, looks for a place to park just as does a newcomer to the drafting department!

To be sure, respect must be earned, not delegated. Leadership comes to those who are followed! They do not inherit authority; they earn it! In the case of Christian leaders, one of God's children becomes a shepherd by first becoming a servant. "Ourselves as your servants for Jesus' sake," said the Apostle Paul (2 Corinthians 4:5). Christians, by the way, might think of VIPs as Victoriously Involved Pilgrims!

Pride is an obvious hindrance to VIP discipleship. So beware! If you invite the Lord Jesus to be the Chief Executive Officer of your life, yet permit pride to blemish your spiritual lifestyle, you can expect to spend time in God's woodshed!

What are the danger areas of pride in our lives? One particular Scripture uniquely and effectively answers that question. Members of the early Christian church in Corinth apparently had over-sized vanity cases, because the Apostle Paul asked them, "Who makes you different from anyone else? What do you have that you did not receive? And if you did receive it, why do you boast as though you did not?" (1 Corinthians 4:7).

When the Apostle asks: "Who makes you different?" he speaks about physical characteristics. Men and women, endowed with physical appeal, sometimes fall prey to the demons of pride. But why? Because God is the One who fashioned us the way we are. Beauty and virility belong to God, not to the humans possessing such endowments!

Paul's second question is "What do you have that you did not receive?" He refers to our talents, our abilities, those positives with which we were born and by which we function and achieve. For these we should be grateful.

But never proud.

In my own case, I sincerely perceive of myself as quite an ordinary person. I recognize my achievements to have resulted from God's blessing on my limited talents. I think He lets me illustrate how our Heavenly Father wants to take people of common ability and less-than-overwhelming physical attributes and touch them with the unlimited abundance of His sovereign majesty. When that occurs—and it can happen to any Christian—humility and gratitude, not pride and flaunting, should characterize my life.

The lead article in the August '91 issue of *Reader's Digest* features Lin Xiangao, whom the *Digest* describes as "the most famous underground church leader in China."

Known to free-world Christians as Samuel Lamb, this man of God spent 20 years in prison for preaching the gospel. Christians come from all over China to ask his counsel on how to give their witness to others.

Yet Pastor Lamb could be missed in a crowd. He stands five feet eight and weighs slightly over 100 pounds. When he speaks, his voice is gentle, his manner retiring.*

He is a vivid example of how God chooses "the weak things of the world to shame the strong" (1 Corinthians 1:27).

Handling pride, along with the desire for VIP status, holds the key to success in becoming a true disciple of the Lord Jesus. Beginning with Lucifer, the highest angel in heaven (see Isaiah 14:12-14), the Bible abounds with examples of how vanity and pride separate people from a vital relationship with God.

Pride was Cain's problem in his relationship to his brother Abel (see Genesis 4:3-7). He could not face the fact that his brother received God's approval while his own offering was rejected. Sounds like Christians vying for VIP status in a local church!

David's brother Eliab accused him of flagrant pride (see 1 Samuel 17:28). King Rehoboam flaunted his royal position causing his people to revolt (see 1 Kings 12:6-11). And Nebuchadnezzar paid the price for his arrogance (see Daniel 5:20). The Lord Jesus Himself clearly identified His disdain for those who publicly demonstrated the ugliness of egotistical piety (see Luke 12:9-14).

No Christian is immune. "If you think you are standing firm," God's word cautions, "be careful that you don't fall" (1 Corinthians 10:12).

I learned the importance of this Scripture the hard way. One day the editor of a prominent Christian magazine came to our plant and asked to see me.

"We're very impressed by your life and achievements," he began, "and would like to feature you in our magazine."

* *Read* Bold as a Lamb, *the Chinese pastor's story, by Ken Anderson, Zondervon 1991.*

"Sort of a testimony?" I asked, a surge of pleasure going through me like a waft of summer's warmth.

"Oh, certainly!" the man replied. "A testimony to be sure! But you are also a man of achievement in the market-place, Mr. Tam, and we want to recognize that fact in our treatment."

I liked that!

"When will you do the interview?" I asked.

"Now if I may."

"Shoot!" I told him. I settled back comfortably in my chair. "Ask me whatever questions you need."

For the next couple of hours, I showed this man my best side. His questions emphasized witness. I impressed even myself through the way I shared some of my more colorful experiences. Two or three times the interviewer himself seemed a bit awed by what he heard. This motivated me all the more.

"It was a great experience," I told Juanita at dinner that night.

"As long as it honors the Lord," my wife said reflectively.

When the magazine arrived with my story, I basked in an aura of emotion quite new to my experience. The copy was professional and appealing, the layout and photographs top notch. I read the article three times in my office that morning and, at home after dinner, read it twice more.

Juanita read it only once.

"I hope it will be a blessing to lots of people," she said.

"I think I should make reprints," I told her, "to give out at my meetings."

I ordered 10,000 copies.

"We'll need 10 days or so," the printer said.

"I really need them for a meeting this weekend," I countered.

The printer looked at the calendar.

"Is that possible?" I primed.

He puckered his lips, drew a light whistle of air through his teeth. "Not without some overtime," he told me.

Overtime? Admittedly, Stanley Tam uses a freshly-sharpened pencil when it came to figuring costs. This circumstance, however, could certainly be looked upon as an exception. I had the reprints in hand for my next Sunday-morning appointment!

Following the message, it pleased me to be able to say, "If you would like a copy of my testimony, help yourself to the magazine reprints available at the back."

I felt a new enthusiasm in my heart as I drove home that early afternoon.

Then I heard that little voice in my heart!

"Why did you pass out those testimonies, Stanley?"

I tried to ignore the question. Wasn't it obvious? I had the testimony printed to win souls!

But the voice persisted.

Again and again. On into the next week. And the next.

When I returned from speaking engagements, when I read my Bible or prayed, the voice persisted like an impolite interruption.

"Why are you passing out the magazine reprints, Stanley?"

Down deep in my heart, I knew the reason. I was advertising Stanley Tam. I wanted to be known as a VIP Christian layman, like the famous industrialist, R. G. LeTourneau, so popular and widely used in his day.

I was proud of what I had done! As I've learned only too well, pride points the way directly into God's woodshed!

I became fretful. I couldn't keep my mind on my work. I tried to rationalize. Might it be I was by nature so unassuming this small incident of personal promotion caused an innocent reaction? I could have settled for this reasoning were it not for one pointed admonition of Scripture that persistently came to my mind: "Do not grieve the Holy Spirit of God, with whom you were sealed for the day of redemption" (Ephesians 4:30).

No physical affliction can be quite as debilitating as spiritual illness. And that was exactly my problem: disorder, heart trouble, indigestion and breathing problems—all of a spiritual nature. On the physical side, I could add insomnia to the list, because the usual repose I enjoyed at night gave way to frequent restlessness.

Although I'm not an exemplary Christian, I am determined to be a true disciple. If I had chosen to live with one foot in the world and one foot in the church, I would have had no problem. The Bible speaks of those "whose consciences have been seared as with a hot iron" (1 Timothy 4:2). Such people have, by disobedience, made themselves insensitive to the still small voice of conscience. By contrast, when a Christian purposely seeks to honor God, the Holy Spirit—in His kindness!—provides a torment of conscience to bring that believer back into line.

One Friday night I was especially miserable. I remembered the words of D. L. Moody, "There is no limit to what God can do with the Christian who will not touch His glory!"

Those words hit me right between the eyes!

"That's my problem, Lord," I cried aloud. "I've taken for myself the glory which belongs only to You! Please forgive me! Cleanse my mind of pride! 'Restore to me the joy of your salvation!'" (Psalm 51:12).

Peace and cleansing came to my heart. What a wonderful experience!

The following morning, Saturday, I went to the office and supply room determined to act on my decision. There I saw a package wrapped in plain craft paper. Without even taking a look at the contents, I scooped it up and threw it in the disposal bin.

At my weekend speaking appointment, my heart was warm and uplifted. I felt that the Lord gave me special unction as I addressed the audience.

"Nothing in all this world is more important than to make Jesus Christ the total Lord of our lives!" I proclaimed. Only Juanita, who sat with others listening, understood how much the statement meant to me that morning.

And, of course, I didn't offer any take-home magazine reprints!

A week later, my shipping clerk came to me and said, "We need to send out silver collectors, but we've used up the instruction sheets that go with them."

"Can't be," I told him. "I just ordered 10,000 from the printer two weeks ago and they've been delivered."

"I don't see them, Mr. Tam."

"Come," I said, heading toward the supply room, "I'll show you."

"All I've been able to find," said the clerk, "are those reprints of that dandy magazine article with your testimony."

"We're all out of those," I responded, adding, "that's for sure."

"We've got a good supply, Mr. Tam. I took some Friday to give out in my Sunday school class. Folks sure did appreciate them."

Whatever was he talking about? Hadn't I destroyed all those reprints with my own hands?

As we entered the supply room, a package from the printer lay on one of the shelves. Stepping closer, I realized I had erroneously destroyed the 10,000 instruction sheets instead of those 8,000 reprints of the magazine article!

Oops.

Should I throw them away again? I'd rather tell somebody the lesson I had learned!

A few days later an evangelist friend came to town and

asked to see me. I told him the whole story. He laughed. I was able to add a slight chuckle of my own.

"Could I see the reprint?" he asked.

I gave him a copy. He read it.

Looking up, he said, "This is good, Stanley." He hesitated a moment and added, "Do you sense that you have victory over pride about this thing?"

"The Lord gave me as good a whipping as I've had in a long while," I answered, "and it took."

"Then why destroy such a fine piece of witness? Use it— not to your glory but to the glory of God!"

Yes, I learned my lesson and have not forgotten it since! As a result, I have spent many hours searching the Scriptures on the subject. I have come to see that pride is Satan's expertise.

In the famous poem, "Paradise Lost," John Milton proposed an interesting theory. He suggested that when the devil was cast out of heaven, he did not accept defeat. Instead, he organized his forces with the intention of setting up a kingdom superior to God's kingdom. No wonder Jesus said of Satan, "When he lies, he speaks his native language, for he is a liar and the father of lies" (John 8:44).

No wonder pride poses such a devastating danger to Christians who seek to honor the Lord with true discipleship. Does this mean God expects Christians to be shrinking violets?

Not at all!

Jesus had an inner circle among his followers. Some 120 believers met with their Lord in the upper room on the day of Pentecost. Among them was a group, 70 in number, especially close to their Lord. In this unit could be found the 12 disciples. Within that was what is called the "innermost circle." It consisted of Peter, James and John.

Where would you be numbered in such a group?

Among the larger group? The 70 perhaps? How wonderful if you could consider yourself spiritual kin to the 12. But then there were the three select ones who accompanied the Lord Jesus to the mount of transfiguration (see Matthew 17:1-2).

VIPs?

You might call them that.

Be sure not to miss the point, however. Business-type VIPs attain status by virtue of their abilities, good or questionable.

By what merit does a Christian move into the Lord's inner circle? None whatever! You and I can become intimate followers of our Savior only by His grace and mercy! (see Titus 3:4-6). If any one thing marks the inner-circle Christian, it is how this person remains very much human while also being touched by the glory of God through obedience to the Holy Spirit's guidance.

I need to select my words very carefully here. To God's glory, and my personal enrichment, I do consider myself to be an inner-circle Christian. But so can any other believer who meets God's conditions!

Satan continues to attack me on all levels. Thank God, for this conflict is to His glory, the win/loss statistics must look very miserable to Satan. The longer we walk with the Lord, the more earnestly we seek to exalt Him in our lives, the more intently Satan will endeavor to upend us. He never gives up.

I cherish the Scripture which assures us of victory. "Thanks be to God, who always leads us in triumphal procession in Christ and through us spreads everywhere the fragrance of the knowledge of him" (2 Corinthians 2:14).

Following the magazine reprint situation, the Lord blessed me with an experience which wonderfully illustrates the inner-circle blessings meant for us to enjoy.

One blustery February night, I drove to Findlay, Ohio, to address a couples' club. Weather limited attendance. Also, audience response indicated this was a more liberal type of church unaccustomed to hearing my kind of testimony. After my talk, people drifted quickly toward the door. Scarcely anyone talked to me. I felt like a stray dog who had wandered into the place. It seemed pointless to have come.

Then, in the parking lot, a woman approached me.

"My name is Shirley," she said, "and I want to thank you for coming to our church on such a nasty night." She hesitated, then added, "But, frankly, both my husband Bill and I aren't happy you came."

"Why aren't you happy I came?"

"The question you asked."

"Question?"

"You asked where we would go if we died tonight." She paused.

I waited.

Then she said, "I know where I'm going." Again she hesitated before continuing with, "It's not to heaven."

What do you do with a lady in a parking lot at nine o'clock? The church is locked but she has a spiritual need. Do you tell her that you hope she finds the way to heaven but, sorry, you need to be on your way home? I couldn't invite her to my car. That's not acceptable ethics, in my opinion. So what to do?

I prayed with my eyes open, asking the Holy Spirit for directions!

Instantly, through my mouth came the words, "Where is your husband?"

"He's in our car waiting. As I told you, Bill's as upset as I am."

"Why don't you and Bill invite me to your house?"

"On a stormy night like this? With you having to drive all the way back to Lima? On these icy roads?"

I insisted, because I was sure she and her husband wanted help.

Well," she said at last, "if you don't mind."

"I don't mind," I assured her.

We went to her car. Bill was clearly pleased with my suggestion.

"Just follow us," he said.

When we reached their home, Bill and Shirley showed me a collection of messages they had received from various radio preachers.

"We read them," Bill said, "but we don't quite understand."

In response, I carefully guided them, verse by verse, through the plan of salvation. It was a struggle. They had many questions. But, as the clock struck midnight, Bill and Shirley opened their hearts to the Lord Jesus Christ!

Obviously the blessed, guiding Holy Spirit had a beautiful purpose in bringing me to Findlay that ugly winter's night!

This couple stuck with their church a few more months but, hungry for good Bible teaching, transferred to another congregation. A year later, I received an invitation to speak at a banquet in the church they had joined.

Bill and Shirley greeted me at the door.

"When I heard you were coming," Bill said, "I asked if I could be the one to introduce you."

And what an introduction it was!

"It gives me much pleasure to introduce Stanley Tam to you," Bill told the audience. "because he is my spiritual father."

A wonderful glow came over me, warming me from head to toe. Was I proud? No, thank God! It was one of my most humbling—and rewarding—experiences.

How very sad that so many Christians become successful in the secular world—VIPs some of them—but choose to remain mediocre as God's children. It is doubly sad when, so clearly in His Word, God shows us how every believer can become an eternal VIP in His kingdom!

"Before his downfall a man's heart is proud," the Bible counsels, "but humility comes before honor" (Proverbs 18:12).

To my way of thinking, the issue is simply drawn. Christians who struggle with pride have yet to learn the difference between VIP status in the secular world and inner-circle relationship with Jesus Christ. The closer we come to Him, the more we realize what the Apostle Paul meant when he wrote, "May I never boast except in the cross of our Lord Jesus Christ, through which the world has been crucified to me, and I to the world" (Galatians 6:14).

The more important Jesus becomes to a Christian, the less problem that believer will have with personal pride!

"He must become greater; I must become less" (John 3:30).

WOODCHIPS

Nutshell

Pride, the foremost nemesis of Christians seeking victory in their lives, cannot be overcome by human effort. Only the Holy Spirit can bring cleansing and a new sense of direction. Closeness to Jesus Christ, through an intimate walk with Him, brings true humility to a human heart.

Branching out

Here are suggestions for overcoming pride and giving Christ first priority in your life:

1. Spend a few moments with Matthew 5:6. Ask God to fulfill this promise in your experience!
2. Permit the Holy Spirit to point out pride problems in your life.
3. Devise some exploratory plans whereby you will endeavor, by God's help, to overcome pride.
4. Do you know a Christian who, in your opinion, demonstrates true humility? Why not ask this person for advice?

11

Your Seven Senses

No eye has seen, nor ear has heard, no mind has conceived what God has prepared for those who love him. 1 Corinthians 2:9

Ever since I began to focus attention on the master-controlled life, I've had a keen and growing interest in Charles G. Finney. I've browsed in bookstores, checked out libraries and read everything I can find on the man and his ministry.

Born in 1792, Finney became an attorney. He had grown up in a secular, if not irreligious, family, giving little thought to spiritual matters until after he signed on as an apprentice with a law firm in Adams, New York.

During his law studies, he discovered numerous authors of legal textbooks frequently quoting the Scriptures, and referring to the law of Moses as authority for many of the great principles of common law. Says Finney in his autobiography, "This excited my curiosity so much I purchased a Bible, the first I had ever owned."

Bible reading matured into Bible study. He saw himself as a sinner but resisted salvation for several years, even rebuffing Christians who told him they were praying for him.

One morning, walking to the law office, he was so taken with thoughts of his spiritual condition that he stopped on the street. "I think I then saw," he states, "as clearly as I ever have...the reality and fullness of the atonement of Christ. All that was necessary on my part was to give up my sins and accept the Lord."

A large tract of timber flanked Adams to the north. In the summer, locals took leisurely strolls among the shaded walkways. Now, brisk October, the trees stood silent. So Finney walked to the woods and entered alone, determined to settle the matter of his eternal destiny.

When he attempted to pray, however, inner pride struck him mute.

"My heart is dead to God," he told himself, "and it will not pray."

Finney would have given up but then, like sunrise, he began to sense the Lord's presence and the reality of salvation for anyone who would believe and act.

"Lord," he cried aloud, "I take Thee at Thy word!"

Thus began a new life for Charles G. Finney!

But this was only the introduction. That same day, after he returned to the law office, he felt as though he looked into the very face of Jesus, so abundant was his new joy.

"I fell down at His feet and poured out my soul to Him," he says. "It seems I bathed His feet with my tears!"

In the next moment, "as I turned and was about to take my seat at the fire, I received a mighty baptism of the Holy Spirit. It was like a wave of electricity going through me. It seemed to come in surges of liquid love, like the very breath of God."

Thus, different from the experience of many Christians, Charles G. Finney received Christ as his Savior and became master controlled by the Holy Spirit—both on the same day. He went on from those moments to become one of the greatest evangelists in American history and a fiery exponent of true holiness in the life of a believer.

Finney reflects, in his autobiography, that he never saw revival come to a church or community without being accompanied by public confession and restitution. He helped people rise above mere doctrinal bias to the experiential relationship God intends every Christian to have with the Holy Spirit.

In facing those with set-in-concrete doctrinal persuasions, Finney sometimes followed an amusing but effective procedure. Addressing Calvinists, he would stress Armenian doctrines and addressing Armenians he would stress Calvinistic doctrines! Above all, he urged believers to seek the cleansing, empowering presence of the Holy Spirit in their lives.

As Alliance preacher A.W. Tozer put it, "In all your getting, above all get unction!" By unction he meant the cleansing, empowering, guiding presence of the Spirit of God!

Why do I relate this historical data?

Not to indicate, for a moment, that everyone should pursue an identical experience. We should never seek to duplicate another Christian's experience.

Instead, I tell this Finney episode as an introduction to what God wants to do for you!

Even in his time, Finney, a Presbyterian, was labeled by some as fanatic. So also today anyone who endeavors to be master controlled faces the likelihood of being misunderstood and at times ridiculed.

But it is truly possible to have a relationship with the Lord just as transforming and valid as Charles Finney's experience.

Take ancient King David, for example. He looked at his body, thought of his mind and emotions, and exclaimed, "I am fearfully and wonderfully made" (Psalm 139:14). From his tryst with the daughter of Eliam to his classical poetry known as the Psalms, this man tasted both the brine and broth of life.

In some instances, David followed the mode of many

today. "If it feels good, do it," say those who pursue hedonism, which the dictionary defines as the doctrine that pleasure is the proper goal of moral behavior.

The hedonist searches for pleasure within the five basic senses—sight, hearing, taste, touch, smell.

In Chapter One, I described the setting of a typical church prayer meeting, where intercession majors on physical and material wants, with spiritual needs often minimized, even ignored. The health-and-wealth gospel, as some call it, enjoys sweeping popularity and acceptance in many areas.

I know what it is like to experience physical healing, to be looking down the gun barrel of bankruptcy and see God resurrect a dying business. But I also know—praise His name!—how much more enriching it is to be spiritually robust and active as a steward of earthly abundance.

My point is that Christian and worldling alike live in the realm of the five basic senses. We enjoy the comforts of modern life. We pursue health and fitness. We relish the taste of gourmet foods. We want to wear good clothes. We dislike poverty and delight in affluence.

We cater to our five senses by the food we eat, the clothes we wear, our choice of recreation and the television programs we watch.

Try an experiment. Monitor conversation outside your church five minutes after the benediction. What do Christians talk about? The sermon? A concept discussed in Sunday school? Or is it the weather, health, sports, politics and a myriad of other secular topics?

You don't have to fit into that mold! You can, if you want, experience a different sphere of life. While the five senses are important, and an intuition-based sixth sense is also helpful, every true Christian will recognize a seventh sense—the awareness of God!

King Solomon described God as having "set eternity in

the hearts of men" (Ecclesiastes 3:11). That is, every person on this planet has an inner consciousness of God. Go to the least sophisticated tribe in the most remote hinterland and you will find people who practice some kind of belief in a divine being.

"Man is incurably religious," someone once said.

Sadly, few Christians have a solid sense of who God is and what He intends to mean to them personally. God tells us in the Bible that anyone who comes to Him "must believe that he exists and that he rewards those who earnestly seek him" (Hebrews 11:16).

You probably believe God exists or you wouldn't be reading this book. But do you earnestly seek Him?

To seek God, you and I need both to believe He exists and also to have a clear view of who He is.

"I see God in the sunrise," I've heard some people say. Others have commented, "When I look into the petals of a rose, I feel as though I am looking at the Creator." Or, "When I watch the tide come in and the tide go out." "When I listen to Beethoven's 'Ode to Joy.' " "When I read Robert Frost's 'Stopping by Woods on a Snowy Evening.' "

All these events are indeed beautiful and inspiring. But anyone whose encounters with God are tied to the five senses has not begun to believe that He exists and that He rewards those who earnestly seek Him!

My co-author visited a Chinese temple early one morning. A lady and her young son also entered. Both were well dressed, indicating a status of wealth. But the woman's face hinted of a need deep in her heart.

She and the boy walked up to the foot of a towering idol. They lit incense sticks, which they placed in a jar so the incense rose to the idol's face. Then the two began to pray, earnestly, almost in tears.

My associate watched, fascinated. This was the first time

he had witnessed heathen worship. Then a voice seemed to say, "That is how big her God is. How big is yours?"

Smitten, he left the temple and returned to his nearby hotel room and his Bible!

Someone has said, "Your God is as small as your doubts and no bigger than the things you worry about."

In actuality, there's only one way to define Him: God is God! If I could define Him in any other way, He would cease to be an infinite being. He is beyond human intelligence, beyond reason, beyond faith, beyond even the Bible itself!

He is God!

Take a small coin from your pocket. Place this coin in the palm of your hand. Think of the coin as the totality of space and time—Earth to the rest of the Milky Way to Andromeda and beyond! Now think of your hand as God's hand, holding in His palm all of space and time. Now close your hand, hiding the coin from view.

Think of God, creator of all things, holding space and time in the palm of His hand, and holding You in His hand, too!

"You will seek me and find me," this eternal God says in His Word, "when you seek me with all your heart" (Jeremiah 29:13).

Are you prepared to search for your own intimate, personal relationship with such a Heavenly Father?

If your reply is yes, then you have just become a candidate for discovering and implementing what I call the Seventh Sense!

Paul told the Christians at Ephesus they should "grasp how wide and long and high and deep is the love of Christ, and to know this love that surpasses knowledge—that you may be filled to the measure of all the fullness of God" (Ephesians 3:18-19). He told Colossian Christians, "We have not stopped praying for you and asking God to fill you with the knowledge of his will through all spiritual wisdom and understanding...in order that you may live a life worthy of the Lord and may please him in every way: bearing fruit in every good work, growing in the knowledge of God" (Colossians 1:9-10).

Those Scriptures speak succintly of this Seventh Sense!

Charles G. Finney discovered and implemented this sense. So have many others of God's children. So may you.

This Seventh Sense is a way of life that breaks free from the five senses and from secular and materialistic values. The Seventh Sense causes a Christian to become a true disciple of Jesus Christ, an eternity person instead of an earthly person.

Does that mean you will become so heavenly minded you are no earthly good, as one wag as stated?

Quite the opposite!

The Seventh Sense enriches your five senses, giving life depth and purpose you have never before experienced!

You remain human. You make mistakes. You have discouragements, up days and down. But the Bible becomes God's contract to you. The Holy Spirit, as your counselor and guide, makes the 23rd Psalm you own experience. You live on this earth, but you walk with God. You are a person of the eternities!

Master controlled by the Holy Spirit!

WOODCHIPS

Nutshell

Most people depend only on their five basic senses, as though life consisted primarily of physical dimensions. The route to happiness and fulfillment for the Christian involves discovering and using one's spiritual capacities.

Branching out

Exploring the Seventh Sense requires discipline and discernment. Here are suggestions.

1. Make sure you avoid any sense of false piety as you consider the Seventh Sense. The devil will confuse and mislead you if he can.
2. Review the Woodchips section of Chapter Eight. Have you activated this wonderful privilege in your life?
3. Do you need counsel? Might your pastor be able to help you? Or you can write:

Stanley Tam
United States Plastics Corporation
1390 Neubrecht Road
Lima, OH 45801

12

Unit One Revival

Jesus said to his disciples, "If anyone would come after me, he must deny himself and take up his cross and follow me." Matthew 16:24

Following a weekend in a church in Atlanta, Georgia, where I had spoken on the subject "God's Woodshed," the pastor wrote to me.

"Something wonderful has happened," his letter began. "For several years, our church has been divided, each faction headed by one of two strong women in our congregation. They always sat on opposite sides of the sanctuary and scarcely ever spoke to each other except in bitterness.

"Last Sunday, as I reviewed your visit with us, the Lord dealt with each of these ladies. Spontaneously, both came to the center aisle. They embraced and, in tears, apologized and begged forgiveness. Our people were electrified. Our church was healed. We now begin a new era in our ministry!"

I don't know the details. I suspect that, when these ladies heard me cite incidents concerning God's woodshed, both could look back upon months—perhaps years—of spiritual dearth in their lives. Each may have been tired of the stand-off, anxious to put their ill will behind them.

Perhaps they exchanged glances across the pews that day as the pastor spoke. Possibly one lady made the first move. The result is that each regretted having waited so long before being cleansed!

I visit 25 churches each year, giving six messages in each. I estimate that half of these congregations enjoy a measure of good spiritual health, which is why they show enough interest to invite me. It's been a blessing to see God honor His word so many times, with people confessing their sins, making restitution and, in some cases, becoming active soul winners.

Even so, I still hear pastors and concerned Christians all across North America talk about the need for revival. The facts certainly support such a concern. In a recent 10-year period of time, Sunday school attendance in America is said to have dropped from 44 million to 25 million. More and more churches have dispensed with Sunday evening services. I know of one congregation where 2,000 attend the Sunday morning worship with less than 100 showing up on Sunday night. Attendance tends to be slack at midweek, if a prayer meeting occurs at all.

Now, obviously, having a Sunday night service does not necessarily characterize a congregation as spiritual. But Sunday night and midweek attendance are surely, in many instances, symptomatic.

Frankly, I have observed a genuine church revival on only one occasion. It took place 40 years ago in the Lima, Ohio, church where I am a member. A missionary leader named Dwight Ferguson came to minister. He combined love for the Word of God with a radiant love for people. Night after night people spontaneously confessed their sins and asked forgiveness for wrongs done. The altar was packed with unbelievers coming to the Lord and with Christians receiving the Holy Spirit's touch.

It was orderly, warm and intense. There were no spectacular manifestations. Just the quiet, cleansing, empowering presence of the Holy Spirit.

I was so moved that I booked a hotel room, to which I retired for hours at a time searching my own Bible on the subject of the Holy Spirit's role in a Christian's life.

"This needs to happen all over America," I said to the missionary.

He nodded. Then a look of pain came to his eyes.

"It could happen," he said quietly.

"Why doesn't it?" I asked.

Dwight shook his head but did not speak for a few moments. "I'll be going to Asia in a couple of months," he said. "What you've seen in your church is happening in many churches in Korea, Taiwan and even parts of Japan. Why don't you come with me?"

I did, and experienced several weeks that changed my life. They opened doors of challenge to my witness and to my stewardship of the Lord's resources.

Many evangelical churches in North America experience numerical growth. Others can be classified as "alive." Yet spiritual vitality wanes among multitudes of believers. More and more Christian homes lack family rapport. Divorce becomes distressingly more prevalent.

Why?

The answer surely seems to be a need for revival!

"Will you not revive us again," the Psalmist prayed, "that your people may rejoice in you?" (Psalm 85:6).

You may have whispered the prayer often. You may have heard your pastor quote it from his pulpit. You may have discussed the need in group Bible studies.

Revival!

Perhaps your own heart anguishes to see a dynamic awakening take place in your church. The fact that it hasn't is no cause for criticism—neither of the pastor, nor of you, nor of the people in your congregation. Instead we need to take a close look at what revival means and, most importantly, how it can relate to you as an individual. A mass revival movement always starts with one person's heart.

You as an individual can experience the blessing of revival in your personal life, even if no one else does! Do you hunger for the Holy Spirit's continual presence? His cleansing? His power? His guidance? All this can be yours!

If you alone among your friends and church were to experience revival, you might miss the rich fellowship that accompanies times of revival. But then, through the witness of your experience, the Holy Spirit might receive invitations from your friends to cleanse and empower their lives!

Look again at the Woodchips section at the end of Chapter Eight. Give some attention to the Implementation material which immediately follows this chapter.

Experiencing personal revival is a launch, not a landing! You will continue growing. You will learn new and vital truths from your study of God's Word. If you are shy, you will find yourself increasingly reaching out to others.

Also, your likes and dislikes will change.

You may look for new associations. You may change social activities. You will develop a reading program helpful to your spiritual life.

And you will fall in love with your Bible!

But you will not reach perfection, not by any means. Nor will I. Let me offer a personal example of my need for ongoing maturity.

My home church in Lima, Ohio, a member of The Christian and Missionary Alliance family, was for many years located in a downtown area. Our community is too small for typical inner-city problems. However, with the development of malls and the move of people away from aging and congested neighborhoods, membership dwindled from 500 members down to 100. So, in the mid-1960s, our people began talking about a new building in a more spacious area.

With such scant membership, financing posed a big problem. Yet everybody felt sure we needed a new church.

Naturally my wife and I discussed the matter. God continued to bless our business. Our giving to missions increased significantly each year. "What would you think, Juanita," I asked, "if we offered to pay for the major costs of a new church?"

"I think it would be wonderful!" my best counselor agreed.

I called our pastor and the chairman of the building committee. Fellow church members thanked us profusely. We, of course, urged them to realize the money was from the Lord who had prospered us so we could share.

I need to explain that, being gone so many weekends of year after year, Juanita and I are a bit like strangers in our congregation. Ordinarily, our voice in planning the new building would have been minimal. But, as everyone knows, money often speaks louder than words.

In the meantime, as the congregation began thinking about a building program, ideas and opinions erupted from all sides. My wife and I try never to throw our weight around. I did have a strong feeling, however, that the building committee was thinking too small.

"Let's plan for growth," I said. "Let's give the Lord room to bless us!"

Even though I offered to be responsible for extra cost, I couldn't get my idea across—especially with the building committee and particularly with the chairman. We didn't come to shouting and insults, but the initial excitement was marred. Many people seemed annoyed by us. My own attitude, especially toward some on the opposition side, likewise didn't please the Lord.

I hope you've never had to sit at Sunday worship realizing spiteful eyes are looking at you and, on your own part, wishing some of those present had stayed home or, better yet, asked for a letter of transfer!

"Why didn't I keep my mouth shut?" I lamented to Juanita.

"People appreciate what you're doing," she said, "but I can sense the jealousy in some eyes."

"I try so hard to have the right attitude about money. Our profits belong to God. We're merely His stewards."

In April of 1966, Juanita and I went to the Philippines where I had been asked to speak at a pastors' conference. "I feel like I'm running away from a problem," I told my wife as we flew across the Pacific, "but it does feel good to get away for awhile."

Arriving in Manila, we were challenged with the realization that busy Christians, whether in the Philippines or North America, often need a fresh touch from heaven. Often we're too busy in church to serve the Lord with our hearts!

"We're praying for a fresh touch from the Holy Spirit," the brother in charge of the pastors' conference explained to us.

As I heard his words, I realized that I, as much as any Filipino pastor, was also needing a fresh touch!

Alone in my room, I went to my knees.

"Lord," I prayed, "use me to bring revival in this pastors' conference and I promise that, as soon as I get back to Lima, I will go to the building committee and apologize for my attitude and the things I've said."

A blessed touch of heaven's blessing came to the conference. Tensions between pastors melted away. One brother confessed bad feelings toward the district superintendent and asked forgiveness.

It was one of the most wonderful weeks in my life!

"Are you going to request a meeting with the building committee?" Juanita asked as we headed home.

"I sure am!" I replied.

But I didn't.

A week passed. A month. Nearly half a year.

Enthusiasm was again soaring among the congregation. Property needed to be selected and purchased. Plans had to be finalized. A fund drive needed to be completed.

I reasoned that if I kept to the shadows, I'd do just as much good as if I apologized. In addition, I was busier than ever with weekends away.

In my mind, I was not at peace. I could blame it somewhat on the fact that my energy waned and I began returning home exhausted.

Juanita urged me to see a doctor, something I had put off for years.

Then, following my address to a statewide women's convention in Lincoln, Nebraska, I barely reached my room when I collapsed on the bed. I made it back to Lima but next morning called our doctor for an appointment.

"You're almost a stranger here," the doctor told me. "I haven't seen you in years. What's the problem?"

"Old age, I guess."

He looked at me skeptically and waited for me to continue.

"My energy's depleted." Trying to be whimsical, I added, "I told my wife I could do the diagnosis myself in four words, 'Slow down, Mr. Tam!'"

The doctor began the examination.

It was as thorough a physical as I could remember. It took several hours. I returned two days later for results.

"We've got problems," the doctor began, his face tense, his voice wavering.

"Problems?"

"We need to put you in the hospital right away for more tests?"

"Why?"

He hesitated. Then he told me of the malignancy that I described in Chapter One. And, as you may remember, it resulted in a trip to God's woodshed! "

"Okay, Lord," I whispered heavenward, "I submit. If I have only two years to live, let them be the most meaningful and fruitful years I've ever known!"

Then it happened!

From the top of my head to the tip of each toe, a tingling warmth encompassed me. I had never known a physical sensation so beautiful. It was like music, like the caress of unseen hands.

"What are you doing, Lord?" I cried out. "Touching me? Healing me? Is that it, Lord? Healing?"

I fell peacefully asleep, not awakening until a nurse came to prepare me for surgery. I wanted to tell her it wouldn't be necessary, but I knew she and the doctor wouldn't believe me.

My heart was overflowing with a doxology of peace and joy!

Later that morning, as I regained consciousness back in my room, I tried to share with Juanita. She was stunned, almost to the point of disbelief.

Then our doctor came.

"This is amazing!" he began. "We've done 18 biopsies, checked and rechecked. Mr. Tam, we weren't able to find so much as a trace of cancer anywhere in your body!"

Master controlled!

For all my humanness, all my weakness, never in my life had I been so confident we really can be master controlled !

"Do you not know that your body is a temple of the Holy Spirit, who is in you, whom you have received from God? You are not your own; you were bought with a price. Therefore, honor God with your body" (1 Corinthians 6:19-20).

Robert Turner, our pastor at the time, came to see me. I told him what had happened.

"As soon as you get back on your feet," he said, "I want you to tell this to the entire congregation!"

All I could think of was facing that building committee, and its chairman in particular!

One Sunday night soon thereafter, I stood before the congregation. We were about three months from finishing the church and moving into the new premises.

"It is true the Lord has healed me of cancer," I began, "but there's another more important healing that needs to take place. I know I've been the cause of this church being divided over plans for the new building."

I hesitated. Silence fell over the crowd, as though the sanctuary were empty.

"Pastor," I said, motioning for him to stand beside me, "I want to apologize for the hindrance I have been. Please forgive me."

Then I beckoned the chairman of the building committee. He came, weeping, and embraced me as he accepted my apology.

Spontaneously, all over the sanctuary, people began making restitution, asking forgiveness, pouring out their hearts to each other and to God. Several, like me, had criticized the building committee. Others had complained about the pastor behind his back. Homes were healed. Enemies became friends. It was wonderful!

After that night, we moved ahead as a united body in our plans for the church facility!

Before this time of blessing could happen, however, one man needed to experience the joy of revival in his own heart.

I was that man!

As I said earlier in this chapter, it's spiritually enervating to be part of a dynamic movement of the Holy Spirit in which multitudes of people experience cleansing and vitalizing personal revival. If such were to happen in your church, however, it would still be a matter of individuals. People like you, as individuals, becoming master controlled by the Holy Spirit.

May it happen!

In your life!

To God's glory alone, I believe He is permitting me to experience aspects of what I call the unit one principle.

For all my weaknesses. And humanness.

But I know how to go beyond my limitations! At the first break of every morning, I lift up the Lord Jesus "in whom are hidden all the treasures of wisdom and knowledge" (Colossians 2:3). I claim such wisdom and knowledge so I may make correct decisions throughout the day. I then ask this for every member of my family, my business staff and each employee. This gives me confidence through the day. I feel that what little success I have made in life is based on this daily practice.

Yes, God is the God of the woodshed, as I have learned from many experiences. But He is also the God of blessing and guidance to those, His children, who are learning to seek His will and to obey His guidance!

If the Holy Spirit is dealing with your heart, if you want cleansing and power in your life, if you want to be master controlled, please turn to the Implementation page immediately following this chapter. Let God do for you what He has done for me, what He will do for any Christian who meets His conditions.

"If my people, who are called by my name, will humble themselves and pray and seek my face and turn from their wicked ways, then will I hear from heaven and will forgive their sin and will heal their land" (2 Chronicles 7:14).

Don't settle for anything less!

WOODCHIPS

Implementation

The following questions and suggestions have been designed to help you more effectively utilize the message of this book in your personal life.

1. Do you wish your life to be master controlled?
2. If your response is positive, review the Woodchips supplements at the conclusion of each chapter.
3. Spend some extra time with the Woodchips section at the the of Chapter Eight. Did you pray the prayer it suggested? If not, would you pray it now? Or, talk to God in your own words, if you prefer.
4. Do not expect some special manifestation to occur. God works in different ways with different people. Your confidence must be in what the Bible says more than in how you feel!
5. Take care so the devil doesn't upend your lifestyle. You must avoid any resemblance to a holier-than-thou attitude. Spiritual pride is a heinous sin! Ask God to help you become a caring, loving, believable human being.
6. Learn now the art of silence. To your dismay, you might find that painfully few fellow Christians are interested in discussing what the Holy Spirit is doing in your life. You may need to show more than tell, as you wait for the Holy Spirit's guidance to opportunities for sharing!
7. Very important! You are at a time of beginning. You are human. You can expect Satan to attack. You will need times of refreshing. You may find yourself going to God's Woodshed!
8. Look to your pastor for counsel. Seek out the fellowship of like-minded friends. If we can help, please write:

Stanley Tam
United States Plastics Corporation
1390 Neubrecht Road
Lima, OH 45801
God bless you!